When Opportunity Knocks

8 Surefire Ways To Take Advantage

When Opportunity Knocks

Knocks

8 Surefire Ways To Take Advantage

Former NFL Wide Receiver
JJ BIRDEN
America's #1 Opportunity Trainer

Copyright © 2015 by JJ Birden
When Opportunity Knocks
8 Surefire Ways *To Take Advantage*

ISBN: 978-1-633-18675-0

Visit JJ

www.jjbirden.com

Connect with JJ
Facebook: JJ Birden
Twitter: @jjbirden
Instagram: @jjbirden
Linkedin: JJ Birden

Printed in the United States of America.

Table of Contents

When Opportunity Knocks

Dream. Reach. Seize. Achieve

Acknowledgements

When you take on a project like this, you don't take it on alone and that certainly was the case here. My support team was made up of the incredible nine members of my family.

To my wife Raina, thank you for your unconditional love, support and all the contributions you made during this journey. It was exactly what I needed.

Thank you to my children and the many times you asked, "how's the book coming?" It was the constant nudge I needed to finish.

LaJourdain J Birden Jr (Son)
Dante D Birden (Son)
Camille A Birden (Daughter)
Justin Birden (Nephew)
LaShawn Birden (Niece)
Brandon Birden (Nephew)
Aaliyah Perry (Niece)
Alishia Perry (Niece)

Last shout out goes to Hassan Kareem and Dr. Will Moreland. Hassan if you had not twisted my arm to attend the training during the winter of 2013 to meet Dr. Will, this book would have never been written. I met the right person at the right time to fulfill this dream of writing my book. Dr. Will thank you for your mentorship and the example you set in inspiring people to reach their "Genius Potential."

Dream. Reach. Seize. Achieve

Foreword

My relationship with JJ Birden began 25 years ago with the National Football League's Kansas City Chiefs in the aggressive and highly competitive world of professional football.

In the Spring of 1990 our Director of Pro Personnel, Mark Hatley, introduced me to a newly signed free agent wide receiver recently released from the Dallas Cowboys - LaJourdain J. Birden Sr.

Upon meeting the five foot ten inch tall 157 pound player, I couldn't help but wonder what on earth our front office was thinking when they offered this young man a contract. At first sight he certainly didn't appear to possess any of the physical characteristics this game of huge men and fierce contact demanded nor did he seem to possess any of the traits necessary to excel at the wide receiver position in the "run first" physically demanding style of offense preferred by head coach Marty Schottenhiemer.

In the previous season Kansas City produced the NFL's premier rushing attack that featured professional football's most dynamic and productive runner - "The Nigerian Nightmare" Christian Okoye. The offensive unit was complimented by the game's most physical blocking wide receiver corps lead by pro bowler Carlos Carson and savvy veteran players

Stephone Paige, Pete Mandley and Emile Harry. In addition, first year players Rob Thomas and Naz Worthing had promising rookie seasons.

Players with a physical presence of size and strength became the profile of the wide receiver position in Kansas City. The addition of the most aggressive and physical receiver in the just concluded 1990 draft, Fred Jones, from Grambling State University seemed to validate the teams intention to continue to covet those same characteristics moving forward.

On the surface JJ Birden appeared to have no chance whatsoever to make the team's final roster. A "camp guy" said the scouting department - someone to run pass routes in training camp to give the veterans a break and keep them fresh. "He has a track background, some speed and quickness", they said, "maybe he can give the defensive backs some good work in practice."

As it manifested itself many times in JJ's life (and, most likely, in the lives of each and every one of us) here again was a situation in which major obstacles that seemed overwhelming were being presented, adversaries who doubted his ability to succeed were present and the task of maximizing his physical, mental, emotional or spiritual potential were in question.

Dream. Reach. Seize. Achieve

In 1990 LaJourdain J. Birden Sr. never wavered. He defied the odds by overcoming those seemingly insurmountable obstacles silenced his critics and seized the opportunity to maximize his potential and realize his dream of playing in the National Football League.

JJ had a plan. He believed in himself and had an uncompromising work ethic. He triumphed in a way that was an inspiration to his teammates and coaches alike. The diminutive figure with the heart of a champion and the character and values of an exceptional mentor and tremendous role model propelled him to succeed at the highest level.

Through his commitment, perseverance and infectious positive attitude not only did JJ earn a final roster spot that year but became a significant contributor to a team that would appear in the National Football League playoffs for 5 consecutive seasons. Despite his stature he became one of the most feared and respected blockers from the wide receiver position in professional football. In addition he concluded his time in Kansas City as the 6th most productive wide receiver in the history of the franchise with 183 receptions, 2,819 yards, 14 touchdowns and an exceptional 15.4 yards per catch - a remarkable accomplishment for an "undersized" player in a game of giants who was designated as a "camp guy" by those professional evaluators who assess talent and project potential for one of the biggest and most successful conglomerates in the world of sport.

When Opportunity Knocks

Reaching our potential thru maximizing our uniquely individual talents is our life long challenge. JJ is an example of one man who was capable of doing just that in both his personal and professional life. In this inspiring book he gives the reader a "blue print" for achieving that same success by recognizing and seizing the opportunities that life's complex journey presents.

This book certainly is not exclusively for the sports fan. Professional football just happened to be a passion JJ had and the National Football League the platform that was presented to realize one of his dreams. The reader will find it speaks to anyone who truly has a desire to succeed, a unique talent to develop or difficult challenge to overcome.

Whether young or old, male or female, amateur or professional JJ's words will motivate, inspire and challenge you to be the very best you can be in every phase of your life. He presents a plan for you to take advantage of those opportunities that can make a positive difference.

It was an honor and a privilege to have the opportunity to observe his plan succeed first hand and to have shared in the excitement and satisfaction of witnessing this special man realize his own potential in one of the most intensely competitive and challenging arenas in the world - professional sport.

Dream. Reach. Seize. Achieve

Opportunity knocked for LaJourdain J. Birden Sr. in the spring of 1990 and he took advantage of it. His book will give you the direction and insight to have the confidence and motivation to do the same.

Al Saunders
Wide Receiver Coach/ Assistant Head Coach
Kansas City Chiefs

When Opportunity Knocks

Introduction

When Opportunity Knocks

It's been a personal goal of mine to become an author. I didn't know when but I knew it would happen at some point. Internally, I've always felt I have something to share. Let's face it we all have a story and each of our stories is riddled with lessons from life. Lessons that if adhered to, by the person that is ready and at the right time could steer them in a positive direction.

The perspective I will share with you comes from years of mistakes, successes, ups and downs and everything in between. I have had a lot of practice at this thing called life, as a husband, father of eight, professional athlete, retired athlete, entrepreneur, man of faith, coach, motivational speaker, fitness enthusiast and a healthy life expert I have been around the block as they say. It's been quite a ride.

When I was thinking about the title of my first book, so many ideas and memories began to surface. I thought back to my days in the NFL when I kept a detailed journal. I had always thought that one day I would share my personal journey of playing in the NFL and give the Fan the inside scope of the NFL. I thought about calling it "Never Quit." I have always had a never quit attitude; I even recorded a motivational CD with the title Never Never Quit. But as a few of my team members and I started to brainstorm we started to notice a pattern. When we listened to my presentations and keynote speeches, we could hear a recurring theme. I would often talk about taking advantage of the opportunities you have in life. Seizing the moment, being ready for your opportunity and not missing the opportunity. We all agreed that my first book had to be about "*OPPORTUNITY.*"

No matter who you are, what your background is, economic situation or your living conditions, we all have opportunities in life. They may come in different forms but we all have access to them. My questions to you are, "Will you seize your opportunities and will you maximize your opportunities?" These will be the main themes of my book. My goal is to share 8 points to help you do just that "**Seize Your Opportunities**" in life. Not just seizing them but totally owning it. Many of us at some point in our lives have missed one, two or more opportunities. I know I have. It's a part of the process. We win some, we lose some, sometimes we make the right decisions and sometimes we make the wrong decisions. There are so many missed opportunity stories I can pull from in the business world. Some which may surprise you for sure. One story I love to share when I'm speaking is the story of the "*Other Bill Gates*" as he's called. Gary Kidall was a software genius who invented the first operating system for PC's in the early Seventies. He missed out on providing IBM with his operating system because he made the choice to go flying instead of meeting with the company bosses of IBM. He missed his opportunity. But there was a wide-eyed young man that was ready and looking for an opportunity to share his operating system with the executives of IBM as well. You may have heard of the little company he runs now called Microsoft. That's right, Bill Gates! Because he was ready for his opportunity, Bill Gates went on to sell IBM his MS-DOS system and the rest is history. I am sure a day doesn't go by that Mr. Kidall doesn't reflect on his missed opportunity.

Our missed opportunities may not cost us nearly as much as Mr. Kidall's cost him, but missed opportunities can be costly never the less. When we miss opportunities, it doesn't make us feel warm and fuzzy. Actually you feel just the opposite. I've heard it said, "One of the greatest pains in life is would of, could of, and should of." Yes that's right, regret! I wrote this book to help you avoid such pains and take full advantage of the opportunities that will come your way.

Looking back over your life, how do you handle opportunities? Do you run from an opportunity? Do you embrace opportunities? Or do you recognize opportunities and take full advantage of them? Whether you struggle with seizing opportunities or have learned to take advantage of opportunities, this book will help you.

When my team and I finally finished brainstorming ideas, I sat down and wrote what you have in your hand, "**8 Surefire Ways To Take Advantage of Opportunities**." I'll share with you 8 surefire ways to seize the opportunities that come to you in life and business, so get ready and enjoy the ride!

What Is Your Passion?

*"Create the Plan, Review the Plan
and Execute the Plan"*

When Opportunity Knocks

The word opportunity can relate to so many areas of life. There can be opportunities, in business, with your family, sports, personal development, faith etc… "Opportunity" has been described as "your chance", the "big break", the "opening". No matter how it's described, I am a firm believer there's an advantage in looking for your opportunity. Some opportunities do fall into your lap, but looking for "**Your Opportunity**" is what I wish to emphasize here. There are certain facets, which need to happen before you can look for "Your Opportunity." It's based on your passion. What's going to provide you that strong feeling of excitement and enthusiasm? What's the opportunity that's going to motivate you to go from point A to point B? These are important questions because they will help you to "**Fully Commit**" to taking advantage of opportunities. Only you know what you want and only you know what you desire. When you discover it, all of your energy, and emotions are locked in as you give it your full attention.

Whatever it is, I need you to get in the mindset of "**Seizing Your Opportunity**." If you're not looking for your opportunity, you're not going to know what to seize. Therefore you must pay attention. I've always considered myself a *student of opportunities*. If it was within my power, I never wanted to miss out on any meaningful opportunity. For you to seize opportunities you have to know what you want, what your focus is or your area of interest. This will assist you in knowing where to look for "**Your Opportunity**." If you don't know what appeals to you, attracts you or what your heart's desire is, you're going to miss out, you'll miss the boat. It's the reason why your eyes have to be wide open and why you must pay attention. Take for instance the day I met my wife Raina. We were both attending the University of Oregon. I was certainly not looking for a wife. I was a two-sport athlete; I was on the football and track teams. My focus was on sports and graduating. However, I knew the type of woman I wanted to marry. I had my future wife's personality and look etched in my brain. So yes I kept my eyes and ears open. One evening, I was doing homework in my apartment and my stepbrother Charles Harris and his buddy Michael Harrison walked in with who would eventually be my wife. The first time I laid eyes on Raina, there was definitely an immediate attraction. I didn't know what she was thinking, and I didn't even know if she was dating someone, so I kind of laid low. Once I received the necessary information I needed after that first encounter, my radar was up and I was looking for the right opportunity to get to know Raina.

And sure enough, that opportunity came a few weeks later when I saw her in the library. I knew this was my opportunity to get to know Raina even better. I was normally a shy person. I did not typically walk up to women and just start speaking to them. But when opportunity is knocking, there is no time to be shy. There was something about Raina and I wanted to get to know her. To be honest I needed to know if she was **"The One"**. Most young men growing up think about the type of woman he will marry. That special woman who will step in and become the most important woman in his life. Your Mom will always have her special place in your heart, but the woman you marry, you'll give your heart to her. With a burning desire to know if Raina was "**The One**", I was not going to allow my typical shyness to prevent me from seizing the opportunity to get to know her. When an opportunity is in front of you, you can't allow fear, doubt or unbelief stop you!

When I approached Raina in the library I pretended I didn't remember her name and until this day she loves to remind me of this. I gave it the old, "What was your name again?" This was all a part of my master plan. After seeing Raina around campus a few times, I was aware she had many guys chasing her and I was not going to be one of them. My plan was to play it cool, but not to the point that I would miss out on my opportunity. Here is a quick lesson; you can't be casual when you are going after an opportunity you believe could be life changing.

I mustered up the courage to ask Raina on a date, I asked her to meet me at the library again so we could study. It was quite a memorable first date. Even though we met at the library there was no studying, I invested the entire time talking to my future wife until the library closed. They had to kick us out. Twenty five years later here we are. Still married and still going strong! An opportunity seized and an opportunity that has produced many happy returns.

Dream. Reach. Seize. Achieve

Looking for "Your Opportunity" is Like Setting a Goal.

You identify something you want then put together a plan to achieve it. <u>Goal setting is part of the routine for high achievers in all professions</u>. It's that extra self-motivation that drives you. The purpose of goals is to help you achieve something that's important to you. Yet, **in order to set a goal, you've got to know what you want.** From there you establish the goals that are connected to this "**WANT**." Many people offer various techniques to goal setting. I prefer to use the **S.M.A.R.T** goals philosophy when it comes to understanding how to set effective goals.

Using the S.M.A.R.T outline, you want your goals to be:

- **S** – Specific, know exactly what you want

- **M** – They need to be Measurable. This helps you to stay on track.

- **A** – Attainable, we want to dream big and aim for the stars but keep one foot securely established in reality.

- **R** – Relevant, they need to be pertinent to your life's reality or sync with your mission.

- **T** – Time Based, goals typically don't get done if there is no timeframe tied to them. This keeps the sense of urgency to accomplish them.

Once you figure this out, then you must establish a plan on how to achieve them. "**A goal without a plan is a wish!**" The two work together and can't succeed without each other. Take the time to write down your goals and make a plan to achieve them. It will be well worth your time. You will thank yourself in the future.

A good place to begin is to ask self-reflecting questions such as:

1. **What do I want? What am I going after?**

2. **What's going to make me happy or what excites me now?**

3. **What's important to me?**

4. **What fuels my fire? What inspires or motivates me?**

5. **What will make a difference in my life?**

6. **What is my WHY?**

Answering these questions will provide you with the focus you will need.

Dream. Reach. Seize. Achieve

An ambitious or motivated person is vigilant and is looking for an opportunity. They know it's going to help them get to where they desire to be. Early on I knew right away what I wanted. I was raised in the inner city of North East Portland. Growing up in the inner city, you always had to pay attention. Now when I talk about the inner city of Portland or let's say "The Hood", you might be asking yourself, does Portland even have a "Hood?" It's a question I have been asked over the years by many of my teammates particularly the ones who lived in the southern states. Some were even shocked to find out African Americans live in Oregon. Several of my former teammates would say, "There's no brotha's in Portland Oregon!" They had images of Portland Oregon being one big suburb with no economic or cultural challenges. Yes we had poverty, low-income housing and high crime. I moved several times when I was young, from apartments to rental houses. You definitely had to lock your doors in the areas that my family and I lived in. Something that still shocks me to this day is that many people especially those who live in the suburbs don't lock their front door all the time. Despite having locks on the doors, we were robbed several times in my neighborhood.

In spite of those difficult situations my childhood was not all bad, I have very fond memories of growing up in Oregon. My stepbrother Charles and I were big into having races in the neighborhood. Every night we lined up on 13th and Killingsworth and raced down the block to Church Street. All the kids in the neighborhood joined us for races. I was the one to beat. I liked to make it interesting by giving my opponents a head start. Even with this lead I would usually win. Those races were so much fun. Our nights were filled with activities, playing hide and seek or having races. It's a bit different than what the kids are doing today. A lot of kids are spending more time sitting on the couch playing video games and being less active.

Growing up in the inner city, I was looking for an opportunity to change my life and my environment. I didn't know how I was going to do it, I just knew an opportunity would arise and I would take advantage of it. Unexpectedly athletics became the "Opportunity" for me to escape the inner city. I say unexpectedly because I enjoyed athletics, my neighborhood was my athletic facility. While playing with my buddies from the neighborhood, I honed my basketball, baseball, and football skills as well as developing my speed. We even played tackle football in the streets. I was content with that. Playing with my neighborhood friends gave me more fulfillment than anything from an athletic standpoint at that time. It was just pure fun. I had no desire to compete for a school or some special program where the competition level was much more intense and the pressure to win was imposed. It wasn't a goal for me at the time to compete on a higher level such as college or pro. As long as I was outside running around with my buddies being active I was good.

Dream. Reach. Seize. Achieve

Around my sophomore year in high school a paradigm shift started to take place with me mentally. Accepting the fact I was not born into a wealthy family, the reality started to set in. The type of opportunities I dreamed of were not happening unless I did something about it. This can be very frustrating when you have big dreams and goals but you don't have the resources to put you on track to achieve them. Let's face it, the reality is, having the right finances can help. There are costs involved. Having the necessary equipment, getting extra coaching, attending instructional camps etc... But what I have found out in life is, when you really desire something, no matter what your economic situation, life will present an opportunity for you to take advantage of. For me, my opportunity came in the form of a free one-day football camp hosted by Oregon State University, also known as the Beavers. This was a huge opportunity; these types of camps usually cost a lot of money to attend. Money neither my family nor I had.

Two things I have to point out, because I don't want you to miss it. Opportunity will find you. And if you are really paying attention it gives you glimpses into your future. How ironic for the rival school of the University of Oregon, where I went to school, would be the school to provide this early opportunity. The Oregon State Beavers is the school that hosted this one-day free football camp at Jefferson High School. Jefferson was located right in the heart of the "hood". No organizations hosted camps in our area. It seemed like everyone else was thinking like me, this was an opportunity of a lifetime, everybody whoever thought about playing football showed up. What's that saying, they were "coming out of the woodwork". Yep the "boys in the hood" showed up and they had "skills."

The football field was packed with local hopefuls! OSU did a great job, it was a first class camp and they made all us feel special that day. There were so many good athletes attending, who could have easily played in college. Of all the wide receivers present and there were many, a guy name Tim and I were the best two. It was obvious and both of us sensed it. We were constantly watching each other and measuring each other's skills. We were thinking who is going to drop the first pass. Neither one of us dropped a pass the entire day. Tim and I became very good friends. He had the skills to play at the next level for sure. I followed his career in high school then lost track after that.

That OSU football camp gave me the confidence that sports could be my opportunity to get out of the inner city and provide me with a better quality of life. For you it could be something else but at the time for me, that was the option I was looking at.

I became passionate about developing my skills on the football field so I would be ready for my opportunity when it came. I wanted to be ready. If you are going to take advantage of opportunities you have to have passion and follow up that passion with a plan that you track with **SMART GOALS**!

Dream. Reach. Seize. Achieve

That camp was huge for my confidence. However, I remember when I knew I was a very good football player. It was the summer of 1981. Often when we played football it was in the streets. The streets were our football field or our field turf. Cars were consistently passing by and the streets were filled with other obstacles. We'd wait for the stream of cars to go by and then we would resume playing. I usually played with my younger brother and his friends. Being I was the oldest and most athletic I played quarterback. Not too many people know this, but I actually have a pretty good arm. Had I been five inches taller Quarterback may have been my position of choice.

One particular day we saw the older kids playing. They were 12th graders who were much bigger than me. I always admired their game and hoped to play with them some day. Odds of that happening were slim. However, on this day, something happened that gave me my "opportunity" to show I could hang with the big boys.

We were sitting on the curb watching them play. At a point in the game one of the guys got hurt. They looked around for a replacement. All of us younger kids were their only option and odds were they weren't going to pick us. Fortunately, one of the guys had seen me play before and said "Pick JJ, he's pretty good". They asked me to play and yes, I was so excited. I saw this as my "opportunity" and I knew I was ready.

When Opportunity Knocks

When we got in the huddle I could tell they were not going to pay attention to me. The QB said, "Just line up and go." Basically it was his way of saying, "clear it out and stay out of the way." So that's what I did on every play, run as fast as I could up the field and stayed out of everyone's way. As the game progressed it was quite obvious they were not going to throw me the ball. My job was to be a decoy taking up space to stretch the defense. I was starting to get a little frustrated because I knew I was good enough to play with them.

I begged the QB to throw me the ball. One of the players said, "Yeah just throw him the ball, we are losing anyway." **Sometimes in life if your "opportunity" doesn't present itself, you have to create it and that's what I was trying to do.** The QB asked me what kind of route I wanted to run and I said, "Just throw it as far as you can and I'll go get it." He looked at me like I was crazy and said, "Ok, whatever!" We lined up, the ball was snapped and the QB took five steps back and threw it as far as he could. I look up and thought wow he really launched it. I hit another gear and went after it. I ran right under the pass and snagged it with my fingertips. Soon as I caught it, I could hear all the guys say, "WOW!" It was exhilarating! When I caught that first pass while running away from the defender covering me, in that instant I knew I was meant to play the wide receiver position. Let me just say it was no longer a secret about my abilities.

Dream. Reach. Seize. Achieve

I scored several touchdowns in that game. I gained instant respect, as they could not stop throwing me the ball. I made spectacular catch after catch. This was the moment I knew I was not an average wide receiver but I had the **"IT" factor.** I was playing with the big boys and I was making it look easy. As a former NFL wide receiver, when people ask me when did I know I was a good wide receiver, this is the moment I share. This confidence booster or as I call it my "Opportunity" catapulted me into playing football the upcoming school year. Not only did I play football but I also ran track during that sophomore year. Later on during my NFL career I ran into one of the guys I was playing football with that day. His name was Ron. I remember him saying, "I knew something was special about you after that game. I have to be honest I did not know you would reach the NFL but I knew you would be good."

Sometimes other people lead you into your passion.

Phil and Carol Walden, were two of the most giving people I had ever known outside of my family. They hosted a local Track and Field club in N.E. Portland called the Albina Road Runners. The club was for the children in the area who wanted to pursue Track and Field. This couple was no ordinary couple they were something special. Not only were they track coaches but also they were like secondary parents to many of us. They went out of their way more than once to provide emotional and financial support for their team members. I can't remember how many times they paid the entry fees to track meets for their athletes because they could not afford the cost. No complaints at all. They frequently made sure lack of funds was not going to be the reason why one did not get to participate. Before many of the meets, you'd see the Walden's car driving around the neighborhood picking up athletes. It was a noticeable old station wagon. That car was always loaded with energetic and driven kids from the hood. Some of the track meets were a few miles away while others were in another State. On those longer road trips, the Walden's assisted in covering food and hotel expenses. That's how the Walden's were, it was all about helping young ones pursue their dreams and they were willing to do whatever it took to make that happen.

There was a popular youth sports camp held at a local small community school Concordia College. The program was free so most of the kids in the area took advantage of it. They opened up their facility and made it available for all types of programs. The first time I went, I was not sure which program I would participate in. After discussing it with some of my neighborhood friends Keith and Kevin Washington, they encouraged me to try Track and Field. The first day of the program, we went right to the track. I remember seeing many of the kids in the neighborhood I was familiar with. Being it was the first day of practice; Mr. Walden wanted to see right away what the new kids could do. After a warm up, he lined us up and had us running 80-meter races. I was anxious to see, how my speed compared with the other athletes. Some of them I knew I was faster than, but there were a few I was not sure about. We lined up and off we went. After about four 80-meter sprints, I had a pretty good idea where I measured. Mr. Walden watched me closely as I ran. I watched him out of the corner of my eye. He was curious to know who the new kid was. After the fifth one he stopped me and said, "What's your name?" I said "JJ Birden." He then asked, "You ever run track?" Not really! I replied. "Okay, JJ Birden, hmmm, he said. I am going to keep an eye on you, you've got some speed. I can tell already, you could be pretty good at this." I was very impressed how Mr. Walden saw the potential in me right away only after running a few sprints. That conversation led to the beginning of my love for Track and Field.

The rest of the summer I ran for the Albina Road Runners. I had so much fun. It was one of the moments in my athletic career where it was all about fun and no pressure. I developed many new relationships that summer. Friendships I have maintained to this day. However for me personally, it was the true beginning of me believing in myself and believing in my potential as an athlete. I put in a lot of training that summer, learning, growing and believing. I have to give a lot of credit to Mr. Phil and Carol Walden, they gave me the "opportunity" and Phil just kept nudging me down that Track and Field path. He'd say "If you put in the time, you could be one of the best to come out of the State of Oregon." The way I saw it, I had to borrow Mr. Walden's belief in me until I believed in myself.

After a few big victory's, it did not take long to have the personal belief.

I guess you could say I was hooked! What flicked the switch? I have to be honest, it wasn't as if I had an ah-ha moment or I was hit with a lightning bolt so to speak, no that was the summer I met Mr. Walden. **I believe many people have had a Mr. Walden in their lives.** An experienced person who comes into your life at just the right time and that person helps to move you down a certain direction.

I'm sure if you look close enough and long enough you will find the Mr. Walden in your life, the right person at the right time to give you that push to help you find your passion!

Do Whatever It Takes!!!

"Discipline, the ability to do, what you need to do, when you need to do it, while no one is watching"

When Opportunity Knocks

I believe the title of this chapter is quite clear and it hits down at the core, "You Got To Want It and You've Got To Want It Badly". This is my second key to seizing your opportunities, **"DO WHATEVER IT TAKES."**

A logical thinker knows that if you want something bad enough, you will do whatever it takes to get it. My former Kansas City Chiefs Coach Marty Schottenheimer used to utter over and over again,

"Men, if it's important to you, you'll find a way to get it done."

Before Coach Marty taught me this, I saw this trait in my mother. Earlier I told you I was raised in the inner city, combine all the challenges that presented and then add that my mom raised us as a single parent. My mom had a **"Whatever It Takes"** attitude when it came to providing for my siblings and me.

I watched how hard she worked and how hard she struggled at times to make ends meet. Although she dropped out of high school her junior year, she never used that as an excuse. She set a good example for us and was not afraid of doing what it took to make sure we had what we needed. While growing up, she held various odd jobs. But the one I remember the most was when she became a welder. You see opportunities can come disguised in different ways. Sometimes people can view them as an opportunity while others might see them as an obstacle.

Through a contact from a friend she was invited to join an apprenticeship program to become a welder for a large company in Portland called FMC. The company was looking for more welders but I don't think they were looking for women. It was not typical at the time for women to become welders for large companies operating on large machinery. Everyone in the family thought my Mom was nuts! I can remember some saying, "Women don't become welders" or "You are going to get all dirty and how are you going to carry all that equipment?" "That job is for men!" Needless to say, my mom did not allow the naysayers to change her mindset. Mom also had key number one, she had a "**PASSION**" for taking care of our family. She saw this as an opportunity to take care of her family. She quickly passed the apprenticeship program and was hired to become a welder at the company. Even after she got the job and worked there for some time, she still had to deal with being questioned whether or not a woman belonged there.

It was no easy job. The best opportunities are usually wrapped in difficulty. The after affects were evident when she returned home. She was worn out! She'd arrive home in full welding attire, wearing big heavy boots. Soon as she arrived, she'd sit down and we would start yanking off those big boots. I can remember my big brother Tony on the right side pulling on one boot, while I was pulling on the other boot. Those boots were so hard to get off. I always thought how difficult it had to be for my mom to walk in them all day long. While we were doing this, my sister TanJa was running her bath water. She was usually sore and very tired so she deserved the relaxation. Mom set a solid example for me in being a hard worker and realizing sometimes the circumstances aren't always perfect. So you make the most of the opportunity set before you no matter what. My mom saw the welding job as an opportunity to provide and that's what she did. We always had the basic necessities for life. She was the first person to teach me to **"Seize Your Opportunity."**

My mom set the standard. With her example, she established a gauge for me to aim for something higher and she better prepared me to handle the unpredictable.

Later in life, I was given the opportunity to put into practice what my mom taught me and what I had seen her do over and over again, go to bat for the family. If you have lived on this earth just a little while, you know that life will throw you curve balls, what I now like to call opportunities. Several years ago I was thrown one of the biggest opportunities in my life. I'm laughing as I am writing this because I can tell you, you have to be careful, because when you first see the opportunity, it will not look like an opportunity.

Dream. Reach. Seize. Achieve

August 2007 I received a call from my nephew Justin Birden. After hanging up the phone, I knew I needed to head Tulsa, Oklahoma to check on my nieces and nephews. Raina and I talked and we both agreed there was a sense of urgency so I took the next flight out to Tulsa. Less than 48 hours later I was knocking on the door where Justin was living. I quickly learned the situation wasn't what I thought it was. I spent the next 24 hours rounding up my five nieces and nephews. The entire scene was like something out of a movie. The police took me to a nearby gas station and told me to wait there. Then thirty minutes later the police returned with two of my nieces and one nephew. I remember one of my nieces Aaliyah entering my rental car filled with tears in her eyes because she wasn't sure what was going on. It touched my heart because I knew she was confused. The following day I was standing before a judge fighting for temporary guardianship of my nieces and nephews. The judge gave me temporary custody of the children.

However, I was required to bring them back 30 days later for a final custody hearing. With 30 days to my next court date I couldn't stay in Tulsa that long, I needed to get back to Oregon. The dilemma was how could I get 6 people back to Oregon in the most economical way. We could drive or purchase 6 plane tickets. Driving was out of the equation; I didn't have the desire to drive. Buying the plane tickets was very expensive. So after talking with Raina, we decided buying Greyhound bus tickets was our best option. I couldn't remember the last time I was on a

Greyhound bus. But our journey was set, Uncle JJ and his five nieces and nephews ranging in age from 6 to 17.

The long bus trip was the most grueling and disgusting form of travel I've ever done. No doubt about it! I'm sorry Greyhound bus service, but I was not impressed. The buses we were on usually had a foul smell. We often sat in the back so we could be near each other. That meant we were next to the bathroom. They consistently overbooked the buses so I was asked several times to allow my six year old niece Alishia to sit on my lap for several hours at a time. Not to mention we observed some pretty quirky people on these buses as well as at the bus station. That actually made it somewhat entertaining as we enjoyed people watching. At the time, I had just started a new job, while my wife and I were still juggling our current businesses.

I can remember making sales calls on the Greyhound bus while Alishia was on my lap. I could not just shut it down, I still had to work and provide for the family. Remember, **"Do Whatever It Takes."** It's interesting to me when people have an amazing opportunity in front of them but they are not willing to put in the effort to achieve it or they allow life to get in the way. I like to share the Greyhound bus story when people try to tell me they can't do something or find the time to pursue their passion. Yeah right! Traveling from Tulsa to Oregon, in the back of a disgusting smelling bus, with my five nieces and nephews while one is sitting on my lap.

What was I doing? Making sales calls! Hey "You do what you have to do when it's important to you."

When we finally arrived in Oregon I'll never forget the some of the first words that came out my wife's mouth. She said,

"You guys stink! Babe, you've never smelled this bad before, oh my goodness. You guys need to get cleaned up fast!"

She was right. We did smell awful!

This was a significant change for our family. Going from 3 children to 8. We were basically like the Eight Is Enough TV show rather than the Brady Bunch. The next 30-days was full of adjustments. We did not have a house to accommodate 10 people, which presented an immediate problem. Without delay, we changed up the sleeping arrangements. My youngest son Dante moved into my oldest son LaJourdain's room while Justin and Brandon took over Dante's room. LaShawn, Aaliyah and Alishia moved into my daughter Camille's room while Camille moved into our bedroom with Raina and me. I get tired all over again thinking about it! We positioned a twin mattress at the end of our bed for her. Despite these drastic changes, my children were great and were willing to make the sacrifice as well. They too saw it as an "**OPPORTUNITY**" to be there for their cousins.

When the 30 days were up, my nieces, nephews and I, headed back to Tulsa for the custody hearing. If you're wondering, we did **NOT** take the Greyhound bus this time. During the custody hearing the judge informed us there were two options for the children's future, return back to my brother-in-law or be placed in separate foster homes. As I'm standing before the judge listening to the dialogue that's taking place, I quickly realized the children's two options were not to be desired. The judge decided it was not a good idea to send them back to their father either so the option was going to be that the children would be sent to foster homes. She then directed a statement toward me that I will never forget.

"Mr. Birden, the court is prepared to send your nieces and nephews to separate foster homes. They will be merged into our system and we will do our best to take care of them. However you are the next of kin so it's your call. You can allow them to go to foster homes or you can take all the children yourself. We will give you full custody."

Interestingly enough I was not shocked at these words, I kind of expected her to say it. But when the judge actually said them, it kind of hit me "right between the eyes." It was "gut check time." Without hesitation I told the judge, "I need to discuss this with my wife." We took a recess and during that time I called Raina. Right away Raina responded "Bring them all home!" She didn't even have to think about it. Talk about "**Seizing An Opportunity**." Now let's analyze this. My wife and I already had three children, yet she had no reservations about adding five more to our family. When I asked her why she decided to take them all in, she says, *"I could not say no. I could not abandon them. My heart could not do that."* Let me just say it takes a rare and special woman to agree to this. We were both on the same page here. There are many remarkable points I could share about my wife Raina, this is one of the reasons I call her, "**Mom Fabulous**!" She is a beautiful woman with a kind and giving heart. One who is willing to put the needs of others ahead of her own. The choice was made and I traveled back to Oregon with all five children and full legal guardianship.

With this newfound opportunity, I was even more determined to build my businesses and provide for my increased family.

When I reflect on this decision, I can't help appreciate the opportunity we were given and the opportunity we took on gladly. We've been able to provide a strong loving and faith based support system for all the children. Providing a new start on life for our nieces and nephews. The only real surprise of this situation was the reaction of some of our family and friends when we made this decision. Instead of supporting us and don't get me wrong many did, but some didn't. They even went so far as to voice their opinion saying we should not have taken these children in. I don't know about you but we both believe that family comes first. Who in their right mind could walk away from that opportunity to impact these young lives and sleep well every night? We could not! I am a firm believer, when it's within your power you do what you have to do in order to be there for family. As I mentioned earlier, some people see circumstances as an opportunity while others see them as an obstacle. Raina and I both saw this as an opportunity to be parents to five more children. To give my five nephews and nieces an opportunity for a better way of life and we welcomed it.

When you are seizing the right opportunity, **it's much easier to become locked in or have "laser focus" if you want it bad enough.** In this case you will not let anything stop you. Barriers, setbacks, obstacles, hurdles are just **"bumps in the road"**.

WHEN YOU ARE NOT FOCUSED
OR COMMITTED

In my 9th grade year of high school I was attending Lakeridge High school in Lake Oswego. I went out for the track team for the first time. Doing so came at a cost. We did not have a normal school bus schedule because of the integration program we were part of; I will explain more about that later in this chapter. If we wanted to participate in after school activities; we had to make our own arrangements to get home. This was no easy task considering the fact that Lake Oswego was about 30 miles away from where I lived in Northeast Portland. Before the ninth grade I didn't participate in any after school activities, but during that year, track and field started to catch my attention. My goal was to get on the 4 x 100 meter relay team. Six of us had to have a run off for a spot on the relay. Only the top four would make it. We lined up at the 100 meters, the gun went off and I finished fifth while my cousin Jeray Bell finished right next to me at 6th. After the race, Jeray and I discussed whether or not we wanted to still be on the track team. Now of course the coach gave us every opportunity to be a member of the track team but at that point it just wasn't important to either one of us so we declined.

You see the obstacles presented a challenge. The obstacle was how to get back home after practice; it was not something I felt like dealing with. If I participated on the track team that meant after practice I would have to walk 30 minutes from school down this long road. Why? That's where the bus stop was to catch the Tri-Met city bus. Then from there, I would take the Tri-Met into downtown Portland, transfer to another bus which would then take me home. Meaning I would arrive home around 8 pm to 8:30 pm. I usually still had homework to do as well. This may have been a "hidden opportunity" but I did not see it. All I knew was I was not on the relay team so the sacrifice didn't seem worth it to me.

Six months later my perspective started to change. I guess you could say my true desire to be successful or my **concern for being "average"** started to burn inside of me. I was ready to put in the effort and make the sacrifices. As I mentioned earlier,

I finally got the bug for Track and Field. I found my two events the long jump and the hurdles.

This was the summer I started to want it. Remember also this was the summer I met Phil and Carol Walden. The next school year, I did make the sacrifice of walking down that long street from Lakeridge High school to catch the Tri-Met bus, into downtown Portland, transfer to another bus to take me home. Arriving home around 8 pm to 8:30 pm every night. I did this my entire sophomore year. Why? The difference was this year it was important to me. I saw the opportunity right there and I was willing to do whatever it took to achieve it. The inconvenience of the walk, bus ride and arriving home late was no longer an obstacle. I knew it was part of the process to get me to where I wanted to be.

I was shocked that as my athletic performances improved during my junior year, it was no more catching the bus. The school started providing me a cab. Yes, they paid for a cab every day to pick me up after practice and take me home. Once practice was over, I went to the coaches' office and called Radio Cab. I think I still remember the number, 503-227-1212. I still arrived home late but arriving home at 7 pm was much better.

My senior year, instead of a Cab ride, one of the coaches or a teammate would give me a ride home. They made sure I arrived home safely every day. I appreciate my coaches Dave Shultz, Tom Smythe, Keith Hurdstorm, Ron Hunt and my buddies Lance Woodbury and Curt Cornick for participating in the "Give JJ a ride home after practice program". When you think about it, there is a bigger story here. **When you commit to those around you, they commit to you.** These individuals were awesome!

The genuine point of sharing this is to highlight the sacrifices I had to make. It was totally inconvenient to not arrive home at a normal hour like other student athletes. Those years taught me a great deal about sacrifice, commitment, and discipline. I was given a clear picture between those who wanted it and those who "truly" did not want it. I was not the only kid from Northeast Portland to have the opportunity to participate in the athletic programs at the Lake Oswego schools. There were other very talented kids, some just as talented as me. However, the difference was they weren't willing to make the sacrifice, and deal with the unique travel situation after practice. "I firmly believe if an opportunity you desire is within your grasp you take it. Nothing should stop you from achieving it. It may not ever come again."

This is why it's so important to choose the right "opportunity." There might be obstacles along the way but to you they shouldn't be obstacles, just speed bumps. "If the "opportunity" is strong enough, the process to accomplish it is easy."

Doing whatever it takes may not feel good at the time, just like working out, you may not like the process, but you will love the results. Over the years I have learned to appreciate the process. Another lesson my mother taught me back in the sixth grade.

I wasn't one of those kids that loved school, I can remember back to those dreadful parent/teacher conferences. It was always the same thing "JJ is great in P.E., extremely conscientious but not very focused on academics. He could be a much better student if he was less of a distraction and focused on his assignments." After hearing this over and over again, my Mother decided it was time to do something drastic. There happened to be an integration program that was occurring in the suburbs of Portland to a city called Lake Oswego. This was a very affluent area, which had very few African Americans living there. The program was built around busing African American students from Northeast Portland to the Lake Oswego schools for their education. Most major cities in the U.S. had similar programs in the 70's and 80's. Once my Mom heard about this program from my Aunts' Joyce and Sandra and that they were close to no longer accepting new students, she immediately enrolled us in the Lake Oswego schools so we could participate. Mom saw this as an opportunity to provide yet again the best for us. Sometimes you take advantage of opportunities, other times you are pushed into them.

Let's talk about hurdles.

I ran the 110 high hurdles in high school and college. I was not the typical high hurdler from a height standpoint, but it was **the challenge of the race that intrigued me**. When I stood in the blocks and looked at those ten 39 or 42 inch hurdles in front of me, all I could think about was how badly I wanted to conquer each hurdle and get to the finish line before my competitors. My focus was not always on winning, of course I wanted to win, but I focused more on proper execution. **Proper execution of my hurdle technique led to victories.** When the gun would go off to start the high hurdle race, I felt like I was being shot out of a cannon. In this particular event, it is not a free run to the finish line. You had ten hurdles and 7 hurdlers there to stop you. During the course of the race there's lots of action. There's never a smooth quiet hurdle race. The banging of the hurdles was the norm. Your competitor on your left or right is hitting you with his arm or leg. The contact during the race was unavoidable and yes it could be a distraction. So your ability to not allow these distractions to take you off your mission is the difference between winning and losing. How can I make this point relative? Think of it this way, the ability to stay focused when facing a test, trial or tribulation in life will be the difference maker for you in "Seizing Your Opportunity."

In my senior years of both high school and college, I never lost a race at Lakeridge or Oregon. I mastered the ability to block out all my competitors and lock in on the goal at hand, which was the finish line. You see when you want something bad enough; you have to become immune to obstacles and distractions. **The ability to focus has always been one of my competitive advantages.** It's probably why I was a good wide receiver too. Catching a ball over the middle when there are guys much bigger who are surrounding you and ready to take your head-off was not a distraction to me. The focus was on the ball, locked in and ready to make the catch. Having a competitive advantage is huge! It's when you do something better than others, you have a talent which makes you more superior to your opponents, contemporaries and gives you added value. Therefore it translates into an **ADVANTAGE**!

Seizing the Opportunity

"Push yourself in your preparation because when it's time to perform, you'll be more than ready"

I played in the NFL for 9 years with a lot of great players and coaches. I could fill up an entire book with just awesome stories and lessons. Maybe my next book will be just about the great lessons I learned on the gridiron.

One great opportunity that came my way was to play with the legendary Hall of Fame Quarterback Joe Montana. Yes, that Joe! One of the greatest quarterbacks of all time.

The year Joe joined the Kansas City Chiefs in 1993; I was probably the most shocked. I can recall being on vacation with Raina and reading in the local papers the possibility of Joe Montana joining the Chiefs. Right away I started to think, "**No way will that ever happen**." Well, two weeks later Joe was a Kansas City Chief. To say I was in shock was an understatement. Joe entered the NFL when I was in the 8th grade. I enjoyed watching his career over the years and always rooted for him. Now you're telling me I will be in the same huddle with him as one of his starting wide receivers? I had to prepare mentally for this. I remember our first practice during the off-season and being in the huddle with him. He was calling the first play, but I was not listening. All I could think to myself was, "That's Joe Montana!"

With a big smile on my face I was like a kid in the candy story. However, reality struck when we ran that first play. The play was X hook so that meant Joe's first pass as KC Chief was coming to me. Yes, I was excited but I was also nervous. I lined up, ran my 12-yard hook route. Before I reached the top of my route, Joe hit me in the back of the head with the ball. Right away I am wondering what the deal is. Joe quickly let me know his game; he said,

"JJ, I don't wait for you to be open. I have already read the defense so I know where the hole is. I expect you to get to the top of your route and get your head around quickly."

Once I heard that, I knew I was playing with one of the great ones. Just that statement alone caused me to step up my game. I became a better wide receiver because of it.

Those two years around Joe I learned a lot. One thing I noticed right away was that he was a confident quiet leader. Not a big talker but he seemed to know when the right time to communicate with the team was. So confident yes, over confident no.

We had no doubt he was the leader of the offense and we had every reason to trust him. One reason why was due to his preparation. Before one of our offensive meetings, I saw Joe studying his plays. The intensity in which he was studying them caught me by surprise. The Chiefs had decided to basically run the same offense as what the San Francisco 49ers ran so that meant Joe already knew the offense. I walked over to Joe and asked him, "Joe, don't you already know the offense?" He responded, "I sure do." I followed up with, "Then why are you spending all this extra time studying it?" Joe in his normal "Joe Cool" fashion said, "Well, I like to memorize all the possible formations so when the offensive coordinator sends in the play all he has to tell me is the play and I automatically know what formation to put the players in. Speeds up the game for me so I can get a quicker look at the defense." Well needless to say, I was impressed and began making a similar commitment. I figured if this guy who's already won four Super Bowls prepares like this, then I need to do the same. Success leaves clues and I was picking them up. And not only picking them up, but learning them from one of the greatest Quarterbacks of all time.

While going through the Cleveland Browns training camp, I faced some top NFL Defensive Backs. My initial introduction to these gentlemen was a very humbling experience. In college, I relied on my speed to get past the Defensive Backs. But when I got to the Pros they were using a technique that allows them to play right up in your face about 1 to 2 yards off, it's called the "Bump and Run Technique." When the ball is snapped, they try and do all they can to get their hands on you and ultimately take you out of the play. If they can jam you on the line, then that was not good. You were no use to the quarterback on that play. I witnessed many speedy and very good wide receivers get cut from a team because they could not beat this technique. During my high school and college days, I had no problem. I was much faster than the guys covering me so I would run around them. However, that did not work when I entered the NFL.

Dream. Reach. Seize. Achieve

Frank Minnifield, Hanford Dixon and Felix Wright were very good Defensive Backs for the Cleveland Browns. They used to toss me around like a rag doll on the line of scrimmage. Weighing 157 lbs at the time did not help me either. I could not get past them. One time, Hanford jammed me so bad he threw me out of bounds and said "This is the NFL little man, you got to do better than that." After being the last WR cut at the end of the Cleveland Browns' training camp in 1989, I spent the next several months perfecting how to beat man-to-man coverage. It was apparent to me if I could not beat bump and run then it was time to fall back on the college degree. **You can't play in the NFL if you cannot beat the Bump and Run Technique. It doesn't matter how fast you are or what great hands you have. Beating press coverage was a must.**

I committed hours of studying other players, walking through different types of releases off the line of scrimmage. I wanted this so bad that I started writing out the different types of releases and even naming them. When you want it bad enough, you do whatever it takes to seize your opportunity. I wasn't going to let the Bump and Run beat me I was determined to win.

Later that season, the Dallas Cowboys signed me. Once I began practicing with them, I continued to perfect how to beat the Bump and Run technique. By the time I joined the Kansas City Chiefs and participated in their mini camp, it was apparent I had improved drastically and was ready to take on the

Defensive Backs (DB's). The DB's knew it and I could see it in their eyes. I was a totally different player and it enhanced my game for sure. This became my **"competitive advantage"** for the remainder of my career.

I learned to utilize my speed, quickness, patience and intellect to beat this technique. It was one of the reasons why I was able to play 9 years at my size. I was extremely good on the line and it was rare when a DB got their hands on me. The respect was there from other DB's in the league. I knew of one particular Hall of Fame DB who refused to play bump and run on me. When they were in man-to-man coverage, he backed off. He once admitted to one of my coaches I was not the easiest Wide Receiver to play the Bump and Run Technique on. It was very satisfying to hear that because it confirmed all the extra work I put in was paying off.

When you have an opportunity in front of you and you are determined in your mind to seize the opportunity, you will let nothing stop you or distract you. Finding your "competitive advantage" will allow you to exploit the opportunity and take full advantage.

Knowing and maximizing your "competitive advantage" is the antidote to the energy vampires. It keeps you moving forward no matter what.

Dream. Reach. Seize. Achieve

Once you have found the opportunity that has caught your attention, the one that hits the right nerve, now the question is are you prepared to "**Seize The Opportunity**."

ARE YOU READY?

This becomes a very important question because sometimes you never know when the opportunity will present itself. Therefore you have to do the necessary activities or the desired actions, as if the opportunity will present itself at any moment. How's that saying go by Henry Hartman, "**Success is when preparation meets opportunity.**" That's what I do as an Opportunity Trainer; I help you prepare for your opportunities.

Every successful person was well prepared when his or her moment came. Do you think Nike Co-founders Bill Bowerman and Phil Knight weren't ready for the Nike explosion? Of course they were! They envisioned it was going to happen. When it did, they were ready. "Anticipation of success is part of the equation." You must visualize your moment or your opportunity. Then walk through it in your mind as to how you would take advantage of it. I did this over and over throughout my athletic career because I never wanted the moment to be too big for me. I already played it out in my head.

For instance, making the big catch to win the game, leaning at the tape to win the Championship race or even making the right suggestions at the right time to close a lucrative business deal. Visualization is a technique that is beneficial for preparing yourself for opportunities. My former NFL Coach Tony Dungy use to tell us

"When you score a touchdown, act like you've been there before."

Realistic anticipation is warranted if you are preparing yourself. Let me say that again, realistic anticipation is warranted if you are preparing yourself. This is very effective. I've tried to do this throughout my life. I've never liked surprises, and I am not very good at being extemporaneous. As a result, I will prepare for something just in case. Call it compulsive or obsessive but I just always want to be ready. Whatever the moment or feat that's occurring, I tried to visualize and replay in my mind what would I do in a given situation or how would I handle it. Then I'd think of the best response for a positive result.

If you can visualize yourself experiencing success, then you are half way there. It still might be necessary to do a little homework just in case. Conversely, if you are expecting something big to happen but are doing nothing to improve your chances of that occurring, then it's a moot point. It's almost like someone looking to get a job working within a community that speaks a different language, but they never take the time to learn the language. I know, ridiculous, that's my point.

Dream. Reach. Seize. Achieve

Let me give you a non-sports related example.

For instance a father who recognizes he doesn't have a strong connection with his daughter. Realizing already he has a very busy schedule, one that's inhibiting him from spending quality time with her. So he's made it a personal goal to seize the next opportunity when she is alone in order to spend some time speaking with her. He's already played this out in his mind, the situation and what he will say to her. He's prepared for it by having conversations with his wife, maybe he has read some books on parenting and he's been practicing the art of asking questions or developing his listening skills. He even put some forethought into what his daughter might be interested in or what topics she might like to discuss.

When the opportunity presents itself the father is well prepared and takes advantage of it. Now imagine him doing this frequently over a period of time. Do you think that this father will be able to build a stronger connection with his daughter? Absolutely! I know this from personal experience. Being a father of eight, actually seven children at home now, there are times I have to look for opportunities to have personal conversations with my children. With seven children who also have busy schedules, it's not always easy to dedicate that one on one time. Looking for my opportunities becomes paramount. When I have these moments with my children, I definitely feel a stronger bond with them. There is a mutual benefit. It's the playing it out in my mind ahead of time, which gives me the advantage and prepares the moment. Visualization is powerful and can be applied in all circumstances.

After years of practicing for my opportunities I have gotten it pretty much down to a science. I find it a lot easier now days to see an opportunity, prepare for an opportunity and SEIZE OPPORTUNITIES. It's pretty obvious what it is you have to do from an athlete's standpoint. Practice practice practice!

Here are some helpful nuggets to help you seize your opportunities.

1. **Knowledge** – Information is needed regarding what you are focusing on so do some research.

2. **Mental** – Mindset is everything. You must be in the right frame of mind to prepare yourself.

3. **Inventory** – Assess the situation and what it's going to involve.

4. **Timing** – There's always a good time and a bad time. Not something you're guaranteed to control but the right time can enhance your success.

5. **Visualization** – See the opportunity surface, see you being ready and executing.

6. **Intangibles** - Patience and stick-to-itiveness, Success doesn't happen overnight.

Working Hard in the RIGHT Direction

"Find your competitive advantage and exploit it"

"There is no substitution for hard work!" This is by far one of my favorite all time quotes.

Hard work is the "**Game Changer**." It's working hard at what you do, giving extra effort to get better. We can want the opportunity and prepare for it, but if we're not willing to put in the work and do what's necessary, it's all a waste of time. One Parable likens it to "**Striving After The Wind**." Trying to grab the wind is pointless just as is seizing an opportunity and not willing to put in the work.

Hard work is what separates the men from the boys or the women from the girls. It's what divides those who are average, with those who are exceptional. I'm very passionate about this subject matter because innately I was never afraid of it. Even at a very young age I displayed the willingness to put in the extra time to get better at something. Even if I saw something for the first time, if it interested me, I wanted to be able to master it.

I can recall when I was about seven years old at my grandparent's home all the family had gathered there for one of our big family dinners, which included uncles, aunts, and cousins. From what I recall a big track and field meet was on TV. It might have been the Olympics. One of the races we watched was the 110-meter high hurdle. It was the first time I had ever seen a hurdle race but once I did, I was hooked.

After the race was over the family went about their business. However, I went into the basement, found some card board boxes, lined them up outside as if they were hurdles and for the next three hours I tried to teach myself to hurdle. I had no clue what I was doing but I did my best to duplicate what I had just seen on television. At some point, one of my family members saw me. They started watching me through the window. Next thing I knew, the entire family was watching me through the window. I remember my Grandmother saying, "Peter Peter" a phrase she used often to express her surprise. She continued, "When that boy puts his mind to it he can do just about anything."

I believe Nike had one of the best advertising slogans of all time to emphasis this, "**Just Do It!**" Don't complain, don't whine, "**Just Do It.**" If you want it bad enough, "**Just Do It!**" When obstacles get in your way, "**Just Do It!**" You're having a bad day, you're tired, frustrated "**Just Do It!**" It might even hurt or you may experience a little discomfort, "**Just Keep Doing It!**" The saying "**No Pain No Gain**" has an insurmountable amount of truth to it. The point is if you give an honest effort, you will never regret it because you know you got better. Getting better and improving your skills, will have a positive effect on your success.

You must work hard to develop and perfect whatever skills are necessary to be efficient at the opportunity you seek. Doesn't matter what it is. Effort is needed. There's nothing in life, which has meaningful value to you that will be easy to acquire. Success is not just going to be given to you. They're not giving it away for free. No, no, no, you have to put in the work. You have to go get it!

When you're diligently putting in time and energy to get better, you're taking steps in the right direction. If you're making the commitment and truly putting your heart and soul into your task at hand, now you're giving one hundred percent. "One hundred percent effort equals one hundred percent results." So it's not about being average, it's about being great.

Let me take you back to the 1991 football season when I was with the Kansas City Chiefs. It was my second year with the team; I was the fifth rated Wide Receiver out of five on the team. The Chiefs did not appear to be satisfied with the lack of speed at the Wide Receiver position. Speed was and is the **"Competitive Advantage"** I had. They continued to experiment with various rotations of players. I did not receive much playing time during that season. It was very frustrating because I had just come off an exciting first year with the Chiefs and was becoming well known as a deep threat. At one point during the season I was averaging 33.1 yards per catch. I ended with 23.5 average yards per catch, which was the most in the league that year.

Despite the frustration of not playing much, let me tell you what I did not do. I didn't complain or become a **"Problem Child"** or cause any kind of disruption within the team. This response is the right response. I've witnessed many players over the years squander their **"Opportunity"** because they showed a lack of patience. Their lack of patience turned into bad attitudes, which led to them becoming a distraction to the main goal of their team.

The teams need for speed became a perfect opportunity for me. I knew this opportunity was too rare and unique. I was not going to waste it. I also knew my time would come. Knowing this, I showed up on time and worked very hard in practice every day. I continuously took copious notes in the meetings and studied constantly to ensure I knew what to do and when to do it. I was confident in my abilities and what I was capable of. I just had to be patient. I did my part to speed up the process. In practice I made sure I performed very well. When the coaches reviewed the films after practice, I was determined to make sure they saw me making play after play after play in practice. At some point, they were going to have to put me on the field and give me my opportunity.

That was my mindset! As I visualized this opportunity becoming a reality, it never crossed my mind that it was going to take the entire regular season for me to be given a fair chance. But it did. My opportunity didn't come until the last game of the season. We were playing the Oakland Raiders. It was already determined that both teams had made the playoffs and would play each other the next week in the first round. Whoever wins this game would get to host the game next week. Playing at home in the playoffs gives a team a big advantage. We needed this win.

During that week of practice I had another outstanding week. Al Saunders our wide receiver coach said "We're going to play you as much as we can on Sunday. You deserve the opportunity, so JJ take advantage of it". I respected Al Saunders. He was one of the best coaches I have ever had. I knew exactly what he was saying, **"Seize Your Opportunity!"**

Do you think I was ready? Do you think I was ready to seize my **OPPORTUNITY**?

You better believe it… I finished the game with eight catches, 188 yards and two touchdowns. Both of those touchdowns were over 50 yards long. If you're not a football person, let me just say that's an amazing day at the office. It was by far the best game I ever had as a pro and yes we did win. When the game was over, reporters were jockeying for position to interview me at my locker. At that time, I was basically an unknown. They asked me, "Did you ever think you would have a game like this?" I responded, "Absolutely, I've been preparing for it!"

So did you catch that response? "I've been preparing for it!"

The results I experienced in the Oakland Raider's game helped my coaches realize even at my size, I was capable of being a starting wide receiver in the NFL. Becoming a starter in the NFL was NEVER my goal. It wasn't something I visualized myself doing. When I thought of starting wide receivers, big athletes like Jerry Rice, Michael Irvin or Chris Carter would come to mind. I know there was Bill "White Shoes" Johnson, Mark Jackson, Gary Clark and today we've got DeSean Jackson and Wes Welker who represent some of the impressive smaller receivers to play the game but I don't think any of them were 157 lbs soaking wet. My goal was just to make it, to prove everyone wrong that I could play. Of course my "**WHY**" or my reason for doing it changed as I realized it was a way to provide for my family. Yet to become a starter at 5"10 157 lbs wasn't something I was auditioning for. I didn't see myself as a starter. When Coach Saunders began the discussions with me about being the starting receiver for the Kansas City Chiefs for the 1992 NFL football season, my reaction was "Come again, are you serious?" It would take me some time to accept this thought. This comes back to the point I shared earlier, you work hard, you do what you need to do, continue to get better and perform at the highest level you won't be denied, unexpected door ways of opportunities begin presenting themselves. Who would have thought as a result of the 1991 practices and because of "**ONE GAME**" or "**ONE OPPORTUNITY**" against the Raiders, I would go on to become a starting wide receiver in the NFL for the rest of my career. Let's break it down this way. There are 32 NFL teams. Therefore making sixty-four starting wide receiver positions available per year in one of the most popular global sports today. I held one of those positions for five years. Yes, I was the little receiver, but with a big and confident heart. It's the beauty of hard work. It can create options and give you choices. I did not see that one coming, but I did embrace and attack my opportunity!

When I was at the University of Oregon running track my freshman year, I was being mentored by one of our senior athletes. He did not know this and may be surprised if he reads this book. His name was Don Ward. Don was a top 400 intermediate hurdler for the Ducks. Right before the track meets began, we would do some speed work. We would do some fast interval training on the track. Don showed me some techniques that I still use today.

Track intervals are when you run short distances on the track and then take a rest and run them again. For instance, after a warm up you may run 100 meters, rest 2 minutes then run 200 meters rest 2 minutes then run 300 meters. You can run these in any variety of ways and on this particular day, we were set to sprint 3 X 300-meter intervals.

By the way, running track intervals is a great way to stay in shape. I still run them to this day, perhaps not as fast though. It's a great workout to keep you in running shape and keep the body fat down. In today's fitness world, they call it High-Intensity Interval Training (HIIT). Now when I put the word "sprint" in the front, it's another way to say you're going to run them fast, and you will be wearing running spikes. Next to running "barefoot" spikes, as we know it, is the fastest way to run.

Dream. Reach. Seize. Achieve

The traction you get with light spiked shoes basically gives you the feeling you can fly. My coach John Gillespie said, "Ok, let's go in pairs." Don Ward was always one of the first to run. He likes to set the pace. He was a trash talker, but a leader as well. He looked right over at me and said, "Hey freshman, you come run with me. It's time to show you how to train like the big boys. If you want to be the best you have to train with the best." I was terrified of course because I was hoping to run with one of the freshmen, but I was never one to shy away from a challenge, so I jumped up and lined up right behind him. When John said go, Don took off. Understand this, I usually run from the front. During my days at Lakeridge High School, I aimed to be the one to set the pace and tried to push our track team to the fastest training times. Not being in the front was unchartered territory for me. All I could see was Don's backside. He was training at a pace I was not use to. About 200 meters into the run I am about 10 yards behind him. I knew he was fast, but I am thinking, "This is just practice, why is he running so fast?" Once the 300-meter interval was completed I fell out on the ground. I had never run that fast in practice before. Clearly I saved my best times for the actual race, not practice. Once I caught my breath, Don walked over to me and said, "That's how you train JJ, if you match your talent with consistent training like that, you will be remembered here at Oregon." The rest of the year I watched Don train at the same level of consistency. I volunteered to run with him whenever the opportunity presented itself. I never forgot what Don taught me. I know for a fact what he shared with me and the example he set during my freshmen year has played a role in any training I have done since then.

"Push yourself in your preparation because when it's time to perform you will be more than ready."

Don was my mentor and didn't even know it, or maybe he did. But we never formerly set up the relationship; I just knew he had reached a level I desired to perform at, so I shadowed him. Don not only had me working hard, but he had me working hard in the right direction.

Tap into the Reservoir of Experience

"Mentorship is a reliable way to reduce the inevitable learning curve"

This is an underestimated part of the equation for success. Many people don't realize the value of having a mentor. The desire to figure it out on your own is admirable, but slows down the process and creates this massive inevitable learning curve. There really is something to possessing experience and maturity. I like the way John C. Crosby described it, he said,

"Mentoring is a brain to pick, an ear to listen, and a push in the right direction."

He's right because when you find the right mentor it can be a "**Game Changer**" and they can serve all the right purposes to helping you achieve your goals and dreams. You don't realize this when you're young because you think you got it all figured out, but none of us do!

When I was young; I looked forward to having my own children. The thought of having my own flesh and blood walking around or "mini me's" was so thrilling. Playing a role in developing and shaping them into adults who would continue the legacy as they raised their own children was exciting to me. I saw it as an amazing privilege. Yet at the same time I was terrified of the prospect of being a parent! "What do I know about raising children?" What can I teach them? I don't know enough to raise a child!" That's what I use to say to myself. Those fears change quickly by the time my wife Raina and I had our first son LaJourdain Jr. By the time we had LaJourdain, Raina and I felt ready, we didn't know everything, but we were pretty confident. As we added two more children we grew and our experience grew as well. There was no situation we could not guide them through. At every stage of their lives we were ready to teach and guide them. With the ultimate goal of teaching them so they would grow up to be successful adults and parents.

The value of being an adult or an experienced professional is hard to measure. So imagine when an opportunity comes your way, one in which you hunger for. If you had access to a "wise and trusted counselor" one, who has been where you want to go and can walk you through the process. Latch on to them as fast as possible.

It's respectable to be self-motivated and independent. All of the high achievers I know, no matter what industry or field have a degree of independence, but they still rely on trusted mentors and advisors. It takes discipline to resist the urge to do it yourself and to use a mentor. I like to describe discipline as "Do what you need to do when you need to do it while no one is watching." It is not very wise to ignore the fact that you don't know everything, and you do need some guidance. Here the word humility comes to mind. Humility has been described as the "Ability to be meek or to recognize you have limitations." It's another way of saying, you realize someone else knows more than you do in this field and you need to learn as much from them as possible.

Having a mentor and being under their tutelage can cut down the learning curve drastically. Their assistance will help you tremendously on your journey. Especially if you have a mentor who's walked a similar path because they know what the journey you're on is like and how to reach the level you're aspiring to achieve. It's a high probability they've learned a few lessons along the way as well. By them sharing their experiences and the lessons learned it can be extremely valuable to you. If you listen, learn and apply you could be on a B-line for success.

The word mentor means "*adviser*" it also means "*guide*." This is very realistic in today's Internet world. You could have a mentor and not even know them at all. The Internet gives us easy access to individuals content today all over the world, therefore making this a strong possibility. For instance, I have a few individuals I follow in my profession I would say are mentors to me. They don't know it, but I certainly do. Some I have been in contact with and have thanked them for sharing their expertise while others don't even know I exist. That's ok because as they keep sharing I keep learning.

Finding mentors who are walking the path you are on is ideal but not always necessary. It is possible to be mentored effectively by someone who has not traveled down a similar road. If they are the "**Right**" kind of example, then they are setting an example you can learn from. Due to their experience in life and knowledge they can still be very helpful. Let me explain it this way. I've had numerous football coaches throughout my NFL career. Many great coaches who made an impact on my career and life. However, I preferred to differentiate them as **"Students of the Game**" and "**Players of the Game**." There were two types of coaches in the NFL, those who had played in the league and those who had not. The coaches who never played in the NFL, I'd refer to as "**Students of the Game**." Meaning they may have played football in high school and college, but never experienced what it was like to play in the NFL. The NFL is a much different game compared to any other level of football. The biggest difference is the "**Speed of the Game**". It's so fast! When you match that with the rate you have to process information and make decisions at the "drop of the dime," for many it can be a challenge. I'd say it's one of biggest reasons why some great college football players never make it in the NFL. Everyone has the physical tools but it's the mental part that causes the separation.

For instance as a Wide Receiver in high school when I caught the ball, I had time to look around to see where the defenders were, then make my move. In College, it was catch and then make a move. However, in the NFL its catch then go and hope you chose the right direction. Usually when you caught a pass the defender was right there battling for the ball against you. You could never run back inside because even the linebackers and defensive linemen were fast. When NFL coaches have not experienced the crazy tempo produced by some of the most athletic individuals in the world, they were at a disadvantage. So they had to spend a great deal of time studying the game and learning as much of it as they could. Watching film or practice doesn't compare to being on the field and experiencing it firsthand. However, through their years of tireless studying and coaching, they would develop a sufficient ability to coach in the NFL despite never playing at that level. That's very admirable!

For the coaches who played in the NFL, they had a little something extra added to their teaching. They were in the trenches; they knew firsthand what it's like. Their input or the mentoring they can provide is incomparable. It's why you see the trend of hiring former players as coaches and commentators has increased. They can provide the personal experience perspective.

Fortunately, I had the privilege of being coached by some of the best wide receiver coaches in the game. John Ramsdell who just retired from the San Diego Chargers coached me at the University of Oregon. Al Saunders who just finished up with the Oakland Raiders coached me during my days with the Kansas City Chiefs. Both of these gentlemen taught me a great deal about playing the Wide Receiver position. Neither played in the NFL but both were successful "**Students of the Game**." I was so impressed with their knowledge of the position. From time to time I would think to myself, "You sure you didn't play in the NFL?"

Dream. Reach. Seize. Achieve

Coach Saunders was great for my career. He was one of the reasons it blossomed. I learned so much from him during the five years I played for the Kansas City Chiefs. During those years, there was only one time where I disagreed with him; normally I pretty much did what he told me to do. Yet one time, I can recall we were going back and forth on something he wanted me to do in a game. It had to do with the Wide Receiver stance and how they should get off the ball. As we went back-and-forth I saw he wasn't going to budge. Even though we had different viewpoints, I reminded myself, I was the athlete and he was the coach. I respectfully complied with his decision, did it his way and moved forward. Sometimes that's necessary when a mentor is mentoring you. You have to shut up, listen and do it! Respect should be given when someone with experience has earned it. Coach Saunders certainly earned it by being a successful NFL coach for many years.

During my journey, I've had many other mentors. A mentor doesn't always have to be older than you. It could be someone the same age and yes, it could be even someone younger than you. The qualifications for mentorship are going to be based on some degree of experience.

I was one of those who was constantly grasping for knowledge. When I reached a new phase of my life if there was something I wanted to achieve I looked to see who the successful people were. Who could I learn from!

Here are 8 tips on how to find the **"Right"** Mentor:

1. What's your goal or what's your passion? – You have to have a starting point.

2. What do you need from a mentor? Spell out expectations of what you're looking to receive.

3. Look for people within your network or look for people outside of your network. – Finding someone you already know has its advantages. The respect is already there and the familiarity strengthens the personal connection. This could cause the mentor to invest even more time in you. The power of the Internet now allows you to be mentored by mentors who don't know you exist. Google search what you're looking for and you will have multiple choices. Social media facilitates the process of tracking and learning from their every move.

4. Find someone who inspires you - No one wants a "deadbeat" mentor. When your mentor speaks they should automatically get your adrenalin flowing and make you want to GO! Remember your going to have those "wall kicking moments" so you need a mentor you can count on to consistently get you back on track.

5. Select mentors with the "Correct" example. Follow a mentor who is at the level you want to be at. They are the living billboard of your desired success.

6. Make personal contact or don't make personal contact - When it's possible show respect and appreciation at all times. Never take your mentor for granted. If you are tracking someone who you don't' have a personal relationship with, there are ways to express appreciation via social media if you so choose.

7. Don't question just do! - "Success leaves clues" a very popular and true statement. There is a reason why you have selected them to be your mentor. They are at a level you want to reach or have the knowledge your looking for. Always remember that and don't question them when they provide exactly what you need.

8. Pay it forward – You had the privilege of learning from someone else. Perhaps they invested time and energy to assist you. Even if you don't know them you are still borrowing from them. Have a willing spirit and share with others. Don't just be a taker also be a giver.

As I am writing this chapter, I'm simultaneously thinking of some of the mentors I've had over the years. I'll share some of the names at the end of this chapter, but let me highlight three specific mentors who impacted my life. Before I do, I need to highlight my Mother Eyvonne Marie Harris. My siblings and I were raised by a single mother. She just about did it all and taught us as much as she could. Mom was a mentor to me in numerous ways so even though I don't include her in the three, it's a given the impact she had in my life.

My Mentors:

Willie Bell aka Mr. Uncle Sonny. My uncle is quite a character. He demanded I call him Mr. Uncle Sonny. I was one of the few nephews who refused to address him that way. However, a few headlocks later, the name became permanently etched in my brain. I think to this day I still call him that. Uncle Sonny was quite talented; he attended the Northeast Portland School Benson High. He was a gifted athlete. I believe he still holds to this day one of the top 100-meter times at Benson High School. He often shared with me stories about how he did not truly reach his potential because he got sidetracked. Although he was one of the best athletes to come out of the state, he missed out on many opportunities. Due to those regrets, he guided me along the way. This raises an important point. Mentors who have failed can be great teachers as well. Their mistakes are learning lessons for future pupils.

My Uncle's mentoring was filled with stories, the challenges, and the decisions he made which he later would regret. He'd share a story and weave in the lessons throughout it. I could clearly see he was trying to teach me something. A few times he would shed tears during those discussions. Those particular conversations were implanted deeper due to his heartfelt emotion. Early on my Uncle Sonny believed in me more than I believed in myself. It's almost as if I had to borrow his belief until I had my own. For example, my senior year at Lakeridge High School after a big football game, my uncle came up to me and said, "You're going to play in the NFL someday." That was the first time anybody mentioned the NFL to me. I was like, "Yeah right". He said, "No you're going to play and I want you to promise me something. I want your first NFL touchdown ball!" **"YOU'RE CRAZY"** was my response. "I'm not going to play in the NFL!" Again he calmly said, "I want your first NFL touchdown ball, promise me that." I said, "Okay you can have my first NFL touchdown ball." Fast-forward to October 21, 1990 the Kansas City Chiefs playing the Seattle Seahawks in Seattle. My third year in the NFL I'm playing near the home crowd from Portland Oregon. My entire family was there for the game. I can recall my Grandmother and Grandfather present too. They walked up some high flights of stairs in the nosebleed section just to see me play. I was told Grandma was out of breath reaching those seats, but it was not going to stop her from seeing her grandson. I was so touched when I first heard that story. I made sure for future games she'd be somewhere in the front row. If you are wondering, the answer is yes; I scored my first touchdown in this game. It was very exciting because you never forget the first one.

When Opportunity Knocks

Once the game was over, I quickly left the locker room to meet my family. I could see my uncle yards away with a big grin on his face walking towards me with his hands out. All I could do was take a knee and give him his ball. You might think I would be upset to have given up my first touchdown ball to someone else, because if you watch professional football, you know a player's first touchdown is a big deal. It's a precious piece of memorabilia. You always see the player latch on to the ball (they don't' spike it) they run to the sideline and give it to the equipment manager for safekeeping. However, for me it was just the opposite. It was a very thrilling moment to give him that ball. All I could think about was the promise he forced me to make back in high school. How did he know? I recalled how ridiculous it seemed to me at the time. My uncle saw something in me I didn't see. He recognized my potential before I did. I was more than happy to give him his reward. I knew I would score many more touchdowns.

My first Touchdown ball traveled around for a little bit. Uncle Sonny kept it at first and then it went to my Grandmother's house for several years. Once she died, it went back to him. Then about 10 years ago he gave the ball to me. It's a special ball with special memories.

My next mentor was **Keith Hurdstrom**, my Lakeridge High History teacher and track coach. Hurd was what we called him. He was a very popular teacher and coach at the school. He knew athletically

Dream. Reach. Seize. Achieve

I had that "**IT**" factor. However, what I appreciate the most about Hurd was how he helped me focus on the importance of academics, not to just rest my hopes on my athletic ability.

"Use your brain" Hurd would say, "Put the same amount of effort into your grades as you do on the track. Your academics will take you a long ways whereas you're limited with your athletic ability. JJ always have a plan B" Hurd would say. His encouragement truly impacted my efforts in the classroom. My grades got better and better and I started winning academic awards. My senior year I was voted student of the quarter. This was an award, which was determined by the teachers. When my name was called during an assembly to receive that award everyone was shocked, even me. I remember some of the brightest students turning around and saying "JJ what's your GPA?" Many of my classmates did not think I was actually doing as well academically as I was athletically. That award was very satisfying because it was the first award I received that had nothing to do with my athletic ability; instead it was based on how I was as a student. Keith Hurdstrom played a major role in those academic accomplishments and kept me more focused on what my brain was capable of not just my legs.

And last but not least was **Kent Baker**, my Financial Advisor. I started working with Kent around my fourth year in the NFL. When I met Kent we immediately hit it off. Kent didn't want to be the type of advisor who made all the decisions for me; he wanted to educate me in a way so we could work together in making decisions for my financial future. He didn't pay my bills or create expense budgets like some advisers have done for players. He made sure I completely understood how to do those things myself. He'd say "You need to have control of your money and the decisions you make with your finances, don't allow someone else to make all those decisions for you." So whenever we would meet it was always a two-way conversation. He wanted my opinion and respected it. To this day my wife and I still work with Kent. He's taught us a great deal about budgeting, saving and how to make your dollar go a long way. One of my goals was no matter how much money I earned; I never wanted to be another statistic, another professional athlete who earns a salary and then blows it all away. Despite what everyone thinks, not all professional athletes are set for life financially. A very small percentage is. Most of us must have a Plan B. However, we do earn more than college graduates so the decisions you make with money determines how far it can take you. Be that as it may, the mentoring we received from Kent helped my wife and I think long-term, he helped us keep our debt down and save. We have stretched our small NFL salary as far as it could go, and Kent's counsel played a key role in that.

I'd like to end this chapter naming some of the other individuals in my life who mentored me in some way. At the risk of leaving many people out, I am inclined to name a few who were mentors for me in some capacity. If I didn't list you and you think I should, then you probably should be on this list too. Nevertheless I can't name everyone.

- George and Josephine Bell
- My Aunts Brenda, Sandra and Joyce
- Tony Bell
- Dan Brewster
- Onelius Jackson
- Vonray Johnson
- Phil & Carol Walden
- Leon Lincoln
- Leon McKenzie
- Keith Hurdstorm
- David Shultz
- Tom Smythe
- Jay Locey
- Dwayne Tyner
- Lance Woodbury
- Don Ward
- John Gillespie
- Bill Dellinger
- Rich Brooks
- Jim Radcliff

- Wide Receiver Coaches, John Ramsdell, Richard Mann and Al Saunders
- Frank Bauer
- Cleveland Browns Receivers group of Webster, Reggie, Brian, Clarence, Gerald and Ozzie
- Marty Schottenheimer
- Joe Montana
- Steve DeBerg
- Stephan Paige
- Bryan Barker
- Sid Devins
- Elias Campbell
- Marty, Jeanette and Andrew Brooks
- Derek Winkel
- Connie Hollstein
- Felix Gudino
- Adam Green
- Jeremy Reynolds
- Jim and Kathy Coover
- Travis Garza
- Ben Stephenson
- Michael Clouse

Dream. Reach. Seize. Achieve

- Lynn Hagadorn and Lisa DeMayo

- Dr. Will Moreland

- Ron Coleman

- Eyvonne Marie Harris

"GO FIND A MENTOR! Once you find them, don't let them out of your sight until their greatness rubs off on you." Be sure to listen, learn and apply. If you already have a mentor, let me ask you this. Can you list them? Can you specifically share how they have helped you? It's a good exercise to do from time to time and see how some individuals have impacted your life so you can pay it forward.

Silence The Doubters

"You can't let everyday life and obstacles stop you from achieving your goals"

Dream. Reach. Seize. Achieve

They're always going to be there. Some people just can't help themselves it's in their DNA. We are referring to the doubters, the dream stealers and negative toxic people. During your journey to seizing your opportunity, you're going to run into these types so you better be prepared. The reasons why they are that way are not always clear. It could be their own insecurities, jealousy or they don't know who you are and your abilities. Think about this, "Not everyone will understand your journey, but that's ok, it's not their journey, it's yours." Use the negativity to fuel you and don't allow it to dictate your path.

It may be easy to evaluate someone by their outside appearance but you can't determine what's inside their heart by just looking at the outside. You can't measure what's inside the brain or what makes one tick. What is your inner driving force? Only you know! Build up your defense mechanisms so when negativity surrounds you, it doesn't become your Kryptonite. Instead it becomes your power source. As the sun is to Superman. Use it as fuel to take you to unprecedented levels.

I entered the University of Oregon my freshman year on a track scholarship. The reason it was a track scholarship was because I couldn't get a football scholarship. When you're 5'10 133 pounds, Division I colleges don't typically recruit Wide Receivers of that size. To be honest, there weren't any Division I football programs recruiting me at all. This was after I was an All-State First Team Wide Receiver. There were some Division II schools interested, but I wanted to play in the Pac-10 (now known as the Pac-12). Instead of getting upset whining and complaining, I converted the rejection into positive fuel. I used positive fuel to drive me into having an outstanding track and field season. At the end of my senior track season, I had many colleges; yes Division I schools, who were recruiting me. As I took recruiting trips to some of these colleges, I'd ask the track coach "What do you think about me playing football?" Most of the schools said no, there were a few smaller schools that gave me the ok but I didn't want to go to those schools. To my surprise, the University of Oregon was the only Division I school who said if I run track the first year they will do their best to see if Coach Brooks would allow me to walk on. "Opportunity!" This was interesting because the Ducks were not recruiting me in football at all, as a matter of fact neither was Oregon State. Well, that's another story.

At Oregon I had a routine, which was typically before going into the weight room for a track workout; I would sneak out and watch the Oregon spring football practices. I'd stand behind the goalpost or sit up in the stands and watch. I wanted to visualize it all. Remember I talked earlier about how important visualization is. That's an opportunity I desired and I wanted to be in this environment as much as I could. The whole time I was watching practice I lamented over the fact that I should be out there, I'm better than that person and that person (pointing to players). I did this several times before being spotted. I had no idea Coach Rich Brooks had noticed I'd been watching practices. Another quick lesson, start hanging out in your desired future, see and go where you want to be in the future. On one particular day, I was standing behind the goalpost. He walked all the way down the field to the goalpost I was hiding behind. I mean literally hiding. Yes, my heart was pounding, and I had nowhere to run. So I tried to make myself skinny hoping he would not see me. That didn't work. He says, "Birden! I have seen you watching practice." He says, "You want to give this a try?" I said "absolutely!" He then tells me to come by and see him tomorrow in his office to talk about it. The next day I go up to Rich Brooks office, and we have a discussion about me playing football this year. Initially, I don't think he was convinced so I had to sell him a little on it. He'd already talked to the track coaches, and they agreed to transfer my scholarship from track to football if I made the team. Then Rich said, and I will never forget this, "If it doesn't work out we will change your scholarship back to track the following year." The point I remember most from that conversation was he never said, "When it works out." I felt at that time Rich Brooks did not believe I could play college football. Perhaps it was a favor for the track coach, who knows. All I knew was,

"Opportunity was knocking and I was about to answer the door."

Entering the fall camp, there were so many receivers on the roster. I was somewhere around 7th on the depth chart. I was so far down I stopped trying to figure it out. As I glanced at the depth chart for the first time, all I could think about was, "You're too small", "You're going to get hurt", "You shouldn't be out there playing", why do you want to do that... blah blah blah blah. These are the comments I heard from many people when they heard about the decision I made to give college football a try. If you allow this negative self-talk to saturate your brain, it can destroy your dream before you even take the first step.

It's self-sabotage vs. self-confidence. Self-sabotage is where your mind is working against you. Have you heard the saying "You are your own worst enemy." This rings true for many of us. It's that inner voice that literally tells you can't do it. You start to believe it and give up all hope. However, self-confidence is just the opposite. You have control over your mind, and you work in conjunction with your heart. You really want it, and your mind is telling you "You got this, go get it!" I was doing my part to add to the positive self-talk. I was in the right frame of mind when I first looked at the depth chart, and my name was near the bottom. It didn't even faze me.

Once again I turned any negative energy into positive fuel and I came out the gate swinging. I made sure from day one in training camp, they would know who I am. Through hard work, commitment and busting my butt, I went from seventh string to second string in a few weeks. I can recall Bob Toledo, Oregon's Offensive Coordinator, coming up to me saying "Wow we never knew you could play like this." I responded, "You never gave me a chance." He said, "Well we were wrong about you, you're going to be a heck of a football player." There are few things more rewarding then when you prove someone wrong and they admit it. Man that felt good.

Early on in life I learned to overcome my own negative and self-limiting beliefs. I was in the third grade at Faubion Elementary School in Portland Oregon. As I mentioned earlier, I was raised in the inner city of Northeast Portland. I attended a predominately African American school. During those years I was a C student, which was considered good in the neighborhood. However I had a major problem with fighting and being a disruption in class. I kind of had that "Little Man's Complex." I was always one of the smallest and constantly felt I had to prove myself and stand out. If I was challenged for whatever reason, we were fighting. Whenever the teachers would say, "Line up here." I'd sprint to the front of the line and was willing to fight my way to be the first person in line. We could have all been lining up to jump off a cliff for all I knew but I was going to be first. I had to be first in everything.

However one time I did meet my match. I got into a shoving match with a very large curly headed 5th grader. One punch to my gut and I was on the ground crying. The kid got in trouble and I was sent to the nurse's office. When I returned home my Mother and Grandma were very upset about this and wanted to do something about it. They didn't even want me to attend school the next day. I did go back and I looked for that kid. As soon as I found him, I walked up to him and apologized. This blew him away! I knew I was wrong and felt that an apology was necessary. He accepted my apology and we instantly became friends. Here's where it gets interesting, I invited him to my house after school. When I got home, this is how I introduced him to my Mother and Grandma. "Mom and Grandma, this is the kid that hit me in the stomach yesterday. We are friends now and everything is ok, can he stay over and play?" I remember both of them standing there with their mouths wide open after that introduction. When you have limiting beliefs or complexes about yourself, they can lead to major problems in your life.

It disappoints me when I meet someone who has all the talent in the world, to accomplish something special. Something they clearly have the ability to do. But later I find out they never did accomplish their goal. Why? They didn't like the coach, they didn't like the teacher, they didn't like their boss, didn't like the person who was instructing them, they could not handle the negativity from family and friends; they didn't like this or didn't like that! To me those are all just excuses. An "excuse is a tool for building a monument of nothing." It has no value at all! They've allowed the dream stealers to take their dreams. Shame on them! Allowing others to dictate your life or dictate your dreams is unacceptable. It's a copout!

Dream. Reach. Seize. Achieve

Al Saunders used to say, "Either you can't do it or you won't do it!" If you want something bad enough as my head coach Marty Schottenheimer used to say "You'll find a way to get it done." No matter what people around you are saying, no matter what they believe or what issue they're dealing with; you know what you can do. Additionally you are aware of what you have to do. You can't allow others to have that kind of control over you. Over the years, I have had teachers, coaches and employers I did not like. I still did not allow my viewpoint of them to stop me from accomplishing what I needed to accomplish. You find a way to deal with the situation, make the best out of it and keep moving forward. The relationship you have with them is only a fraction of your life. So never let that get in the way of your opportunity.

I've done a video series of motivational coaching points on one of my YouTube channels (www.jjbirdenspeaks.com) the one, which fits this point, is Coaching Point #14, "**Control What U Control**." There are times in life people become too concerned about stuff they can't control. You can't control other people's attitudes, you can't control their belief systems, you can't control their efforts and you can't control what they think about you. Nonetheless, what you can control is what you do every day. You control your choices. When Joe Montana joined us during that 1993 season there was so much negative press out there about his ability to continue to play at the highest level. He was coming off an injury, had not played for some time and he was 36 years old.

Did he allow such talk to bother him? Nope! I witnessed his consistent determination and preparation every day. That's what he could control and he did. His game time performances were impressive. That first year, he led us right to the AFC Championship game. One game before the Super Bowl! I'd say he silenced the doubters right away.

It's always best to keep a positive outlook on life. People who know me have heard me say or seen in my email signature or social media posts "**Stay Positive**." A very popular phrase I got from another mentor of mine Vonray Johnson. Vonray taught me a lot about fitness, health and staying positive. Keeping a positive outlook on life is another way to build up your defenses to handle the doubters. There's so much negativity in the world today. It's hard to even watch the news. Such negativity can suffocate you. By having a positive outlook you always see the bright spot in every situation. Even if things are bad there should always be something to focus on that is positive. The simple fact I am alive and breathing is enough to keep me positive. Every day you wake up is another day to accomplish something special. You get a "**Do Over!**"

Recall the words at the beginning of this chapter "Not everyone will understand your journey, but that's ok, it's not their journey to understand, it's yours." "Don't let negative, toxic people rent space in your head… Raise the rent and kick them out!" Silence the doubters make them go mute!

Dream. Reach. Seize. Achieve

You never want to permit anyone to crush your dreams or allow "**Energy Vampires**" to get you off course. Energy Vampires are deadly when it comes to crushing dreams. They're also known as "**Dream Stealers**." What are "**Energy Vampires**"? I like the way Jen Nicomedes describes them in her *MINDBODYGREEN* Blog, she says:

"Energy Vampires can be your family, friends, clients, colleagues, teachers, neighbors, lovers, or even strangers. And they come in all types...

- There is the blamer, who lays blame on everyone else without ever taking any responsibility.

- The guilt trippers use shame to get what they want.

- Jealous bees can never genuinely feel happiness for anyone else.

- Then there are the insecure ones, who pull others down to their level of low self-esteem.

- The fun haters seem unable to embrace joy. The bullies stomp on the little guys to elevate their egos.

- **The Debbie downers, the whiners, the short-tempers, the gossipers, the drama queens, and the list goes on..."**

I am sure we all know people who fit right into some of these categories. Energy Vampires can suck the life right out of you, crush your passion and destroy your dreams. So if at all possible, you want to avoid them at all cost. Try to hang around positive people as much as possible. People who share your enthusiasm and will give you the sincere support you need to go after your dreams. They will support you no matter what!

Show Up!!!

"Dream Reach Seize Achieve"

We could call this the "**Put Up or Shut Up**" chapter. Yes, there has to be a time when you've got to "**SHOW UP!**"

Everything we've shared thus far is aimed to help you "**Seize Your Opportunity**." All the tips and coaching points have led up to this chapter. I've shared how you need to find your passion. You want it and believe you deserve it. You've prepared and worked hard to make sure you're ready. A skilled mentor has been guiding you along your journey. No dream stealers are going to stop you from achieving it. So when you get your opportunity, what are you going to do with it? The simple answer is "**PRODUCE!**" You've got to perform and make the best out of your opportunity or as my good friend Dr. Vernet Joseph says, "**Live To Produce or Be Replaced**."

You see I don't desire you to just seize it, I want you to be "**GREAT**" at your opportunity. Who wants to be average? Your desire should be to perform at the "**Highest Level**" so you need to own it.

A huge part of showing up is how you prepare. Your preparation can make all the difference in you winning and losing in life and business. Thinking back to my NFL days, I remember how much homework I received. Yes, each night we as players had homework.

Dream. Reach. Seize. Achieve

Sometimes your edge going into game day was based on how much film you watched of your opponent and the player who was covering you. Just to give you an idea, my second year with the Atlanta Falcons, we were set to play the Dallas Cowboys. Deion Sanders, the Hall of Fame Defensive Back known as **"Prime Time"** was coming off an injury. He'd make his season debut against us.

Deion was the best corner back I ever faced and I played against many great ones. Deion was so gifted athletically. If he made a mistake, he always had the ability to recover. Sometimes it was on purpose because he was known to bait the quarterbacks to think the wide receiver was open. When the QB threw the ball, Deion would close fast on the ball and usually knock it down or intercept it. Many of those interceptions turned into "Pick 6". He'd take it to the house and score a touchdown. I had never played against Deion so I studied a lot of film on him before the game; I wanted to be ready for my opportunity to **"SHOW UP ."**

I was trying to figure out his weakness, I'm not sure Deion had any. However, after watching many of his previous games I picked up a tendency of Prime Time. Deion loved to play the bump and run technique and he was very good. He played in your face and talked a lot of trash. Yet he liked to favor one side because he refused to let you beat him outside. By preparing and studying, I was able to come up with a few releases for him. Remember, I had worked hard to beat the Bump and Run

Technique. When game time started, it was apparent that Deion had already commanded so much attention we did not throw the ball his way. It was another facet of his game that was so amazing. Sometimes the QB's pre-snap read was **"Where is Deion?"** From there they threw the ball away from him. Big advantage for the Defense because Deion covered one section of the field on his own. I experienced this first hand, because during the first half of the game I was not thrown a single pass.

Never one to waste an opportunity, I figured I'd use the time to practice my releases against Deion and kind of drive him crazy. So that's what I did. I ran all over the field making him chase me everywhere. Even when I knew I wasn't getting the ball. If it was a running play, I would still run a Go route, which was straight down the field as fast as I could. Every time Deion figured out what I was doing it was too late. At one point he said, **"C'mon JJ!"**

In the fourth quarter my opportunity finally came. It was 3rd and goal, and we were on the 4-yard line. The play was X-Slant, so the ball was coming to me. I knew exactly what I was going to do. Given that I knew Deion played head up but protected his inside, I had a plan to make him think I was going outside then I'd come under him. It was a gamble but according to my film preparation it should work. When the ball was snapped, he was about 2 yards in front of me. I stuttered my feet in place then took two hard steps outside to get him to think I was running a fade route outside. Right away Deion took off outside to stop my fade and as soon as he did, I planted on my left foot and came inside under him to run the slant. I thought to myself, "**IT WORKED**! I am open Bobby Hebert", our QB at the time, "**THROW ME THE BALL**."

For some reason Bobby didn't throw it in the first hole when he should have so I kept going. I saw his arm come up and then he released it. I immediately locked my eyes on the ball and started tracking it. I will be honest, for a fraction of a second; I thought to myself "**I AM GOING TO SCORE A TOUCHDOWN ON "PRIME TIME**." As soon as my hand went up to make the catch, I could feel his presence. As I reached up, Deion's hand came right over the top and knocked the ball away before I could catch it. "How in the world did he recover so fast?" But he did, and that's why they called him **Prime Time**! He **SHOWED UP**!!!

View it from this perspective. You may have patiently waited for your opportunity for some time. Perhaps you were overlooked or passed by. You could have been dealing with circumstances, which prevented you from initially accomplishing it. There comes a time when you need to show others you're worthy of that opportunity. You need to own it and hold on to it. This is that time!

I have seen many people in my life who have worked so hard for an opportunity. One they wanted so badly. They've put in the time and effort to get it. But when they got it they were not prepared, they couldn't produce and lost it. Perhaps it was due to a lack of confidence or they didn't have the right preparation. I've seen people put into positions where they had huge opportunities and they didn't know how to take advantage of them. I am a firm believer when these moments happen; you've got to have a plan already in place. Alfred A. Montapert put it this way,

"To accomplish great things we must first dream, then visualize, then plan... believe... act!"

Former NFL Coach Tony Dungy, who was a defensive back coach while I was in Kansas City, used to tell us; "Visualize yourself making the big touchdown catch. So when you do score, you can act like you've been there before and not make a fool of yourself in the end zone." Familiarity of your moment increases your ability to produce. Adding a plan with it is "**Icing On The Cake**."

Many people can "talk the talk but can't walk the walk." Can you back it up? It's one of the qualities, which amazed me about Deion Sanders the NFL Hall of Fame Defensive Back. He was quite the talker on the field. I remember him talking that entire game! My strategy was to say nothing. The entire game I ignored him and just kept running those "**Go routes**" on him. In the fourth quarter when he finally realized I wasn't going to say anything, he said, "JJ you are about the quickest and quietest mouse I have ever played against." I looked at him and just shrugged my shoulders and he started laughing. He may have done lots of smack talking during his career but he backed it up. He commanded respect on the field. **Prime Time** always produced.

It's hard to fake it too. For those who do, at some point they get exposed. I tried to do that back in the fifth grade at Applegate Elementary. I really wanted to play in the band but I had no musical talent what so ever. My dear friend Dan Brewster who was a very experienced musician, had an extra trombone and said he would give it to me if I would take lessons to learn how to play. Of course I said yes. The very next day I went to band practice and told the music teacher not only could I play the trombone, but I could also read music. He immediately put me in the band to see what I could do. I sat down and when the band members started playing I just blended in. I had no idea what I was doing but started playing. Now when I say, "playing" I mean I was just making noise trying to pretend I knew what I was doing. When the class was over the music teacher said nothing to me. I thought for sure I had pulled it off. The next day I did the same thing. I blended in making noise and I thought I had fooled them again. Moving the telescoping slide mechanism back and forth like I knew what I was doing. However, after the end of the class, my teacher asked to speak to me. He said, "I think it might be a better idea for you to play the big drum. Just hit it once or twice and you'll be fine." I was really disappointed and shocked he would make such a last second change. It took me years later to put two and two together. I was exposed. The music teacher could tell I was faking it and I was not able to produce any pleasant music with my trombone. You can't fake **SHOWING UP!!!**

That was a life lesson I will never forget. I told myself I would never fake it again. I would put in the work to be one of the best.

In life you will always be rewarded for putting in the work. It may not look like it at first, but be patient and you will see in the long run that it is not worth trying to cut corners.

Here's a formula I use for my clients and myself. It has helped me to be ready to produce:

- **Create the Plan** – You have to have some kind of strategy in place.

- **Review the plan** – Go over it a number of times to see if it makes sense.

- **Execute the Plan** – Now it's time to put your plan into action. Have the courage to do so. You might be nervous or afraid but that's okay, you still need to go out there and just do it.

This has worked for me to make sure when the opportunity did come I was ready to produce. How does this formula work in real life, let me explain. During the track season of my junior year in high school, I was having another really good season as a hurdler and a jumper. I was going into the district meet as a favorite in the long jump, triple jump and high hurdles, but the intermediate hurdles was a newer event and I wasn't quite there yet. Our top intermediate hurdler Thane Cleveland was top ranked in this event. He was also on the mile relay team. We had three really good runners on the relay but needed one more to have a shot to win the District meet. Thane came up to me the day of the mile relay final and asked me if I would run the last leg for them. My immediate response was, "**Are You Crazy**!" First, I had never run a 400-meter and had no desire to do so. Not to mention the fastest guys were always on the last leg. I knew for certain the guys I would run against were all seniors and much faster than me. Apparently coach Hurdstrom had already cleared it. It was my call. Thane assured me "By the time you get the baton you will have a 30-yard lead, I promise you that. All you have to do is finish it, take it home and don't let anyone pass you." I started to think about it; I probably wasn't going to make it to state in the intermediate hurdles and the relay team did have a shot if we could finish in first or second place. Would you call this an obstacle or an opportunity? Definitely an opportunity, I was just a bit terrified because it was unchartered territory for me.

I thought about it for a few more moments, and all of a sudden my mind said, "Let's do this!" I am not sure why but the competitive juices started to flow. I knew it would be a challenge, but it was a challenge I wanted. I told Thane I'd do it. Shortly after that I started second guessing the decision when

I noticed the 200-meter final champion, the 100-meter final champion, 400-meter final champion and all of the runner-ups were running the last leg. If I lined up with each I am sure they would beat me in a flat out race. I had good speed but I wasn't at their level yet. I was going to race these guys in the last race of the meet.

It's race time and here we go. The race started and as Thane had promised, they did exactly what they said they would do. The first two guys ran great legs. They were awesome! Thane ran the third leg and he continued to extend our lead. While I was watching Thane come off the final turn, I formed a plan. It was obvious I was going to have a 30-yard lead. Since I could not beat these guys in a head to head race I figured it was best to let them catch me on the backstretch. By the time they do catch up, they should have used up quite a bit of energy running me down. Therefore, I should have a little left in the tank on the final stretch to beat them. That was my plan. I reviewed my plan over and over and it seemed to make sense. Now was time to execute the Plan.

On the final anchor leg, I get the baton first with a big lead. I took off at a moderate speed, but in a very controlled stride. I can remember hearing my track coach Keith Hurdstrom yelling, "**Go faster go faster**!" Others were saying, "**He's going too slow**." But I just ignored everyone because I was going to "**Stick to the Plan**!" By the time I got to the middle of the first straightaway here comes the 200-meter champion Greg Wills. I could hear his fast strides reeling me in. As soon as he caught up to me I said to myself, "Hey it's about time Greg, I've been waiting for you." He immediately tried to pass me, but I would not let him. I picked up my pace and ran stride for stride with him. I kept him on the outside therefore forcing him to run a little bit longer than me in lane 2. By the time we came off the final curve here comes the 400 m champion and the 100 m champion. We were coming down the straightaway, all in a line. It was crazy exciting! I look to my right I saw everyone there and I could tell they were a little tired. My plan was working to perfection. The only concern I had was would I have anything left. Well it was as if I downshifted to gather myself and simultaneously up shifted to a faster gear. I was off and running! I pulled away just about two strides in front of everyone with about 70 meters to go. This must have been a great visual for the audience because each of us was in a lane burning down the home stretch. I gave it all I had the last ten meters. I was able to hold them off and crossed the finish line with a Team victory. It was the first time I ever raised my hand when crossing the finish line. It wasn't normal for me to show such excitement, but I was very proud of myself. I can still remember Thane grabbing me and hugging me so tight I couldn't breathe and I started hyperventilating, I had to hit him on the back with the baton so he would let me go. That particular race taught me a great deal about myself. That is, it's okay to be scared. It's okay to be afraid. Yet don't be too afraid of an opportunity that you run away from it.

Again, you form the plan, review the plan and have courage to execute it. Lock in on the "**EXECUTE**" part. Anyone can put a plan together, but it takes great courage to have the guts to follow through with it. If you do this with wholehearted effort, whether you win or lose, you'll be satisfied. If I had lost the race at the end, I still would have been proud because I executed the plan to the best of my ability. Fortunately in this case I won. It was a moment I have never forgotten and still fires me up to this day and serves today as the most exciting moment in my entire athletic career.

GOOD THINGS HAPPEN TO THOSE THAT SHOW UP

There have been many unexpected perks I never dreamt about, like being placed on football cards and in video games. Now that was cool! The first football card I was on was the 90 Plus Club. This card was made for any player during the 1990 season that scored a 90-yard touchdown or more. I had the privilege of achieving that against the San Diego Chargers on the 3rd play of the game. Steve DeBerg threw me a perfect pass. I could not believe the play worked exactly the way our coaches said it would. It brings to mind the first fan coming up to me asking me to sign it. I was so taken back and kept starring at it. I said, "Where'd you get this?" The fan could see I was so excited about my first card; he gave me the extra one he had.

Dream. Reach. Seize. Achieve

I enjoyed signing autographs and can honestly say I never wanted to tell anyone no! I enjoyed the fans. I felt that if they were willing to come out and watch us or support us in any capacity, the least I could do was sign my name, which took all of five seconds to do. Now there were some times when the timing was off. Perhaps I had to get to a meeting or somewhere in a timely fashion. It was hard to say no, but there were times you had to.

When Joe Montana arrived, I learned a trick, just follow Joe. When the crowds would see him, they'd forget about the rest of us and converge on him so fast. You'd hear "Joe, Joe, over here." That was an easy and less guilty escape to my destination. I remember one day spending an hour practicing my signature so I could sign faster, but still make sure it was legible. I finally figured out how to connect those two J's then the B. Whenever I signed something that Joe was signing as well, I would sign right under his name. I am sure you know why.

When my career ended, I think I ended up with 39 individual football cards. I know this because whenever a new card of ours was released, the card company sent us each 100 of that particular card. I am not 100% certain I have 39 because recently, a fan sent me a card to sign for them and it was one I had never seen. So there could be a few more new JJ Birden cards floating around out there I'm not aware of.

Video games! I am on a video game, no way! That was my reaction when Tecmo Bowl came out. Tecmo Bowl was the video game that launched video football to its heights today. Madden football video games clearly dominate today, but Tecmo Bowl started it all. I loved that first video game because they made me so FAST in that game. Bo Jackson and Christian Okoye were unstoppable in the game, but I could run like the wind. I was flying all over the field. Playing a game where you could throw yourself the ball was special. I know now game systems let you create your own players. To me, that's just not the same. The only problem with the Tecmo Bowl game was if you threw the ball to me too much I would always get hurt. Ugh! I blamed it on a glitch in the programming.

The players were into those games big time! The fans weren't the only ones who enjoyed them. We often had tournaments at the practice facility, training camp, or while on the road traveling for away games. It was common for one of us to host a tournament. These were fun times and less pressure. If you didn't like what you saw you just hit "reset." No coach is going to yell at you for that, but your teammates would never let you live it down.

I am impressed that Tecmo Bowl Football lives on to this day, twenty-four years later. There are actual Tecmo Bowl leagues. I have met some of the participants on social media. They've informed me I am still tearing it up on the game and fast as ever.

NEVER SHY AWAY FROM PUTTING IN THE WORK

I recall in high school, pushing myself through my own workouts on Howell's Hill in Northeast Portland. Howell's Hill was a famous hill named after a local athlete name Byron Howell. Legend has it he ran those hills nonstop on his own all the time. It led to him being the first Oregon high school athlete to win the 100 and 200 meters three years in a row at the State Track meet. That hill was the barometer I used to challenge myself. When I wanted to push myself and test my will, I went to Howell's Hill. Many times I ran the hill, on the weekends and while it was raining. I'd ask myself mid-way through the workouts, "Is this really worth it? Why am I doing this?" Yes self-doubt can creep up on anyone, but I would quickly brush those thoughts aside and focus on what I was doing and why I was doing it. When the last run came, I always ran my hardest. To me, it was about finishing strong. I felt it was a true test of "How bad do you want it." I prefer to express it this way and this could apply in all areas.

"Anybody Can Do It When It's Easy"

I would tell myself anyone can run these hills in perfect beautiful weather, with fresh legs while others are running with you, however it takes a true champion or a true professional to run these hills on the weekend when you could be sleeping in, on his own, in the rain and after running 11 hills while making your last one your best. You always make the last one the fastest! This was a test of mental toughness. When it comes down to it, a great deal of it was mental. Just as easy as it is to talk ourselves into doing something we can quickly talk ourselves out of doing it. Although the hill usually kicked my butt it was so worth it. It was the extra work I put in to be the best.

Did showing up for those early morning workouts pay off?

Those Howell's Hill workouts along with the many other extra Saturday workouts I did during my senior season enhanced my competitive edge and allowed me to come within ½ inch from winning the High School State track meet my senior year by myself. Yes, I did say by myself. We had many outstanding track and field team members from Lakeridge High school participating that weekend. Shout out to all of them because they gave their best effort. However, had I not lost to my long jump rival and buddy Chris Bolden by a ½ inch, (24'10 1/4 to 24' 9¾) I could have achieved something that still hasn't been achieved to this day at the 6A level in the state of Oregon. Be that as it may, the University of Oregon came calling with a full ride track scholarship. Yes, I'd say the hard work paid off. It was worth it!

SHOW UP FOR YOUR OPPORTUNITIES!!!

Stay Hungry!!!

*"Never forget what it took
to get there"*

What has helped me is maintaining a mindset of **"STAYING HUNGRY?"** I have a consistent desire to get better. I might be at an advantage here because my height and size caused many to doubt me and I never forgot that. When I became a starter in the NFL, I knew they wanted a taller and bigger receiver. Knowing that drove me to work harder and harder and to never give them a reason to replace me. I used to have a comic strip in my locker. It was a picture of the starting line in a 100-meter race. At the start there was a turtle, rabbit, horse, man, and a cheetah. The cheetah said, "Here we go, I have to prove myself again." I love that quote because I knew every day I would have to prove at 5"10 157 lbs that I belonged there. This attitude carried over into my preparation and training throughout my career, to the point of it becoming habitual. It was rare for me to miss an assignment as a player. They could always count on me. Coach Saunders use to say, "Be where you're supposed to be when you're supposed to be there." You can rest assure I was always there. To me that was about **"Owning Your Opportunity."**

This as well as reflecting on all the challenges I went through in my life helped me to maintain the right frame of mind. Recalling the struggles and remembering what it was like reminded me of why I was doing what I was doing. Growing up in the inner city made me want to break the cycle.

At a young age I noticed many who were comfortable being locked in the **"CYCLE"**. The cycle that sometimes locks in those who are raised in the inner cities or the "**Hood**." I did not want to be in the cycle of struggling and living from paycheck to paycheck, having to get food stamps to get by. Going to the laundromat to wash your clothes because you could not afford a washer and dryer. Having one pair of gym shoes to last the entire school year knowing at some point a hole in the front toe would appear. Shoe glue and I became best friends. I would frequently try and repair the inevitable hole. Shopping at discount grocery stores where they sold food very close to the expiration date. Sharing a bedroom with my brother and sister. Don't get me wrong, as a single parent my Mother was great. We always had food on the table and a roof over our head. However, I didn't want to live like this the rest of my life.

How about the cycle that locked you in your neighborhood, rarely giving you the opportunity or the desire to leave that city or state.

I had a desire to travel and see more of the world. Many around me were content with this life cycle and seemed to have no desire to break it. Not me! I was determined to break the cycle. *I was not content with being average.* I wanted more! I saw the same thing over and over again. I wanted something different. Sometimes in life, you know what you don't want before you know what you want. Albert Einstein said the definition of insanity was "*Doing the same thing over and over again and expecting different results.*" My plan was to heed his advice. Seizing the right opportunities I felt would create different avenues to explore and provide me with options. I was not desperate and would still rely on my principles; I wasn't going to go just after anything. As long as it did not compromise my family, faith, integrity and my passion, I was all in!

In one of the professions I am in we describe it as your **WHY**?" WHY are you doing what you're doing? **The "WHY" is the motivating factor for your focus on the goal or in this case the "Opportunity."** If you know what your **WHY** is or your reason for doing it, it motivates you constantly to take the steps necessary to accomplish it. Through the good days and bad days, you keep pressing forward. If you don't know your **WHY** or your reason for doing it, then you better figure it out. When faced with obstacles if the **WHY** is not there to keep you focused, more than likely you will give up and quit!

Motivational speaker and Publisher of SUCCESS Magazine Darren Hardy in his CD **"Making the Shift—Your First 7 Days, Developing the Entrepreneur Mindset"**, has an effective way of describing the power of knowing your "**WHY**." He uses the example of walking across a plank. He says, "If I had a plank that was 10 inches wide and 30 feet long and offered you $20 to walk across would you do it? The plank is only one foot off the ground." Most people would because it's not very difficult and that's some easy money to earn. He goes on to ask, "What if I took that same plank and made a roof top bridge between two 100 story buildings with it. If I still offered you the $20 dollars for walking across the plank would you do it now?"

At this point no one would do it. The risk factor involved is not worth $20 dollars. Now Darren makes it interesting, he says, "Now imagine if your child is at the opposite end of that building and the building is on fire. The flames are licking at their neck and if you did not walk across the length of the plank to save them, they certainly would perish and die. Would you walk the length of the plank now? Without question and immediately, $20 dollars or not." Why would a parent finally walk the length of the plank? The risk and danger are still there. Their reason for doing it has changed. Any loving parent at this point is going to be more concerned with their child's safety and not their own. They would sacrifice their own life to save their child's life without much thought. What happened here? What was the difference? The parents reason for doing it or their "**WHY**" became more important. This is the point of this analogy and really brings this point home. If the "**WHY**" is strong enough, nothing should stop you. You will be **HUNGRY**!!!

Do you know what your **WHY** is? Think about it. Then answer this, what are you willing to sacrifice to get it? Are you willing to give up your time, energy and finances if necessary? How about giving up some time with those you enjoy spending time with? Are you committed to follow some type of program, which might make you uncomfortable but pushes you to your limits? These are progressive logical questions. To achieve success, sacrifices must be made. All great achievements come at a cost so you might as well mentally prepare yourself to give up something. Sacrifices in connection with your preparation can give you the right results.

There are countless stories of high achievers, those we admire, and who have had to make sacrifices in order to perfect their craft. I am sure Pablo Picasso did not become a great painter overnight. Muhammad Ali wasn't labeled the Greatest without any effort and we know the Wright Brothers who are credited with the first airplane flight in 1903, sacrificed a great deal to achieve their goal. They dedicated hours on this project starting back in 1896. The point is there will be small sacrifices while other times the sacrifices will be large. It's all relative, but well worth it.

Honest self-evaluation can be extremely helpful here. The key word is "**HONEST**." There were different aspects of my NFL career when I had to take honest evaluation of my performance and say to myself, "JJ that is not good enough". For instance there were times when I was playing with the Atlanta Falcons, I was not happy with my performances. I dealt with many hamstring injuries during those two years, which truly affected my performance. It was constantly beating up my confidence. I often wondered if I should have taken the Chicago Bears offer instead of being in Atlanta's highflying offense. One game vs. the Jets during my first year, I can recall watching game film with my teammates of the defensive back I'd be playing against for the up-coming game. They all agreed I was going to work him over and have a big game. I knew it too. He was no Deion Sanders and for sure I was going to be on ESPN's Sports Center. I ended up having the worst game of my life and I was embarrassed. Talk about eating a big slice of humble pie. It was one of the few times I allowed overconfidence to get the best of me. I learned my lesson fast and went back to the basics in my preparation. I went back to work! I vowed that would never happen again. I went back to being **HUNGRY**!!!

I received this poem below from one of my early football coaches. It has always helped me to appreciate the power of self-evaluation.

The Guy in the Glass Poem
(Man in the Mirror)

"When you get what you want in your struggle for self, And the world makes you king for a day, Then go to the mirror and look at yourself, And see what that man has to say. For it isn't a man's father, mother or wife, Whose judgment upon him must pass, The fellow whose verdict counts most in life, Is the man staring back from the glass. He's the fellow to please, never mind all the rest, for he's with you clear to the end, and you've passed your most dangerous, difficult test, If

the man in the glass is your friend. You can fool the whole world down the pathway of years, And get pats on the back as you pass, But the final reward will be heartache and tears, If you've cheated the man in the glass".

By Dale Wimbrow, first published in The American Magazine in 1934.

These words make you think about the man in the mirror. You can't fool yourself, you know if you're doing right or doing wrong. You know if you're giving your best effort or dogging it. If you are not finding success in your endeavors, be honest with yourself. Are you the reason? There's always a reason why. We might not always like the answer, but there is always a reason. It takes a true champion to admit it and then make the adjustments.

Over the years I've met all types of athletes. The ones who combine these three qualities are the ones you often hear about; they are **Skill, Talent and Hard Work**.

Let's break these down for a second because they do matter in your ability to maximize your opportunities and to stay hungry:

• **Talent** is just that natural ability you have. This special ability is inborn, is part of your genetic makeup. Some say it can be classified as that certain flair or instinct you have. The reality is you are gifted with this talent.

• **Skill** is the ability you have to do something. It's been developed due to practice, and training. Skills are often taught and the more you practice them the better your skills become. There is a relationship between skills and talent. Talent can be a first step to enhance a skill. A skill can be a polished ability when merged with talent.

• **Hard Work**, I hope by now you understand it. However this time, let's use the Webster's dictionary to define it. "Hard work is working energetically and devotedly; hard-working; diligent."

The individuals who are able to combine all three are the high performers. No matter what their area of focus is, they clearly finish in the upper echelon. This is not just in sports; it certainly could be applied in the business world or even in academics. Talent you can't control. Either you're born with it or not! However skill and your ability to work hard you can do something about. Let me illustrate it this way.

Let's take math. After many years of taking math, I reached the conclusion some just have a natural talent for understanding mathematical concepts and equations. It was a subject I passed, but it was always a struggle. I never truly could get the concepts. Especially in the Calculus classes I took at the University of Oregon. My last term of science calculus was the hardest class I ever took. I would invest hours at night working on one problem because I just did not get it. Trust me when I say, I did all I could to understand it. I sat in the front row of my class and paid attention as best as I could. When class was over, right away I was asking questions to my math teacher. I even briefly had a tutor. Still to no avail I did not get it. So what did I do? Realizing I lacked this natural ability for math or at least these advanced classes, I practiced those formulas over and over. I'd spend hours going over them. I still did not get it, but most of the time got the right answer because I memorized the formulas and just followed the steps to solve them. It was so frustrating, and more than once I received help from my cousin Dwayne Tyner and another buddy of mine Stevie J. Those two were very good at math. They would go over the problems with me and explain what I was doing wrong. I'd look at them with amazement and go "huh!" I'd say to myself, "how in the world do you understand this?" But they did and they excelled in Math. The true lesson for me was to not give up. This diligence paid off when I received a B minus on the final, a class I needed to pass in order to graduate. It was one of my most proud academic moments in college. I was aware of the sacrifices I made to get that B minus. I put in the work and got the results. I was hungry or maybe just ready to graduate!

Stay hungry and keep the passion, focus and keep the intensity going, I want to leave you with 8 guiding principles to help you:

Dream. Reach. Seize. Achieve

1. Remember why you started in the first place.

2. Challenge yourself from day to day.

3. Have a consistent "success" routine of preparation.

4. Get an accountability partner.

5. Consistent Self – Evaluation

6. Reflect on past achievements. (video, photo, memory)

7. Sticky Note Motivation – Find a motivational quote or an affirmation, which inspires you. Put it on a sticky note and stick it somewhere you will see it constantly.

8. Prepare and perform as if you are going to lose the opportunity.

Maintaining the fire, the passion and drive will keep you at the top. Take these guiding principles to heart. Aim to get better. You never stop learning and never stop getting better if you can hold true to this, you'll be **UNSTOPPABLE** and seize and maximize whatever opportunity you want!

This is JJ Birden signing off. Hoping you're ready to "**Seize Your Opportunity!**"

About JJ Birden

Born and raised in NE Portland Oregon, JJ attended Lakeridge High School in Lake Oswego, Oregon. He earned a track & field scholarship to the University of Oregon. After running competively his first year he begged Oregon's then head football coach Rich Brooks for a chance to "walk on" the football team. He was determined to show coach Brooks that even at 5'10" and 150 lbs, he could play college football. JJ made the team that year and is considered the first track star to successfully walk on and excel at football for the Oregon Ducks. He continued to stand out in both football and track & field during his remaining years at Oregon.

JJ was a standout track & field athlete, winning all Pac-10 and All American honors his junior year and qualifying for the 1988 Olympic Trials in the long jump. He was recently inducted into the Oregon Athletic Hall of Fame as part of the Oregon Ducks 1985 NCAA Championship Track & Field team.

JJ was drafted in the 8th round of the 1988 NFL draft by the Cleveland Browns. After the draft he attended the Cleveland Browns rookie camp. Following a promising start, he suffered a knee injury, tearing his ACL during the third practice. The injury immediately ended his track career.

Since JJ was only one internship away from graduating from the University of Oregon, the

Dream. Reach. Seize. Achieve

Cleveland Browns invited JJ to complete his internship by working in their public relations and sales departments that Fall. JJ graduated from the University of Oregon in 1989 with a Bachelor of Science Degree in Sports Marketing.

Football

Playing in the NFL was not part of JJ's dream. He rested his hopes on making the 1988 Olympic Track & Field team. However, after the knee injury in the Cleveland Browns rookie camp, his attention moved towards the NFL. He went on to have 9 successful years in the NFL playing for such teams as the Cleveland Browns, Dallas Cowboys, Kansas City Chiefs and the Atlanta Falcons.

JJ played with some of the best players who ever played the game, such players as Bernie Kosar, Troy Aikman, Ed "Too Tall" Jones, Derrick Thomas, Marcus Allen and Joe Montana. When asked what was the highlight of his career, JJ responded, "It would be the 1993 season with the Kansas City Chiefs. Two special things happened that year, we made it to the 1993 AFC championship game and that was the year I got to catch passes from one of the greatest Quarterbacks to ever play the game, Joe Montana." JJ retired from the NFL in 1997.

Family

JJ married his college sweetheart Raina DeLeon in 1990. They have 3 children together, LaJourdain Jr. (24), Dante (22) and Camille (19).

Due to JJ's NFL career the Birdens have lived in various cities: Lee's Summit, MO; Suwanee, GA; and Tigard, OR. They now reside in Scottsdale, Arizona.

In 2007 JJ unexpectedly received a call from his nephew in Tulsa, OK. The following day he was on a plane to Tulsa, to check on his 5 nieces and nephews. During this visit, JJ discovered his nieces and nephews were to be placed in foster homes. After consulting his wife, they were awarded full guardianship of the children, Justin, LaShawn, Brandon, Aaliyah and Alishia. He brought them back to Oregon (where they were living at the time) to live with them.

Although some have questioned the Birdens' decision to go from a family of 5 to a family of 10, JJ says, "Sometimes you have to do what you have to do to support your family. Raina and I cared about our nieces and nephews and could not see ourselves abandoning them." To this day there is never a dull moment in their household. They are a close-knit family who strive to put family and spirituality first, which they believe has contributed to an exciting and happy family life.

An Inspirational Keynote Speaker

A natural born speaker, JJ has the ability to touch the hearts of his audience. He not only motivates, but moves listeners to action by offering sensible and successful ways to perform at the highest level. He's passionate about helping others seize their opportunities in life. He incorporates the perfect balance of a refreshing presentation mixed with real life experiences of a husband, father, entrepreneur and professional athlete. In any given presentation, he could be sharing lessons from experiences from being bussed outside his neighborhood to segregated schools in an upper class suburban area, unexpectedly adding his sister's five children to their family, the doubts that circulated as a small man (5'10 and 157 lbs) entering a big man's game (the NFL) or perhaps lessons he learned from the greatest quarterback to play the game: Joe Montana.

JJ's speaking career began during his rookie year in the NFL. He has spoken in front of all types of audiences, from children to adults in the athletic and business world. His ability to tailor his message will benefit all types of listeners.

As a speaker he is not one to put your audience to sleep. His dynamic and lively approach will captivate your audiences. JJ says, "I was once told by a professional speaker, 'If your presentation doesn't have fire, then put it in the fire!' So you can believe me from the moment I begin speaking, my goal is to lock you in right away and hold your attention until the end."

Keynote Speaking Topics:

- Team Building Success
- The Mindset of a Winner

- Life Success
- Underdog Success
- Network Marketing Success
- Success, Marriage and Family
- The Opportunity Gene
- Never Never Quit

Dream. Reach. Seize. Achieve

Interested in having a unique, engaging speaker at your event?

Contact Information:

Phone- 480.824.8318

Email- info@jjbirden.com